Benjamin William Arnold

History of the Tobacco Industry in Virginia

From 1860 to 1894

Benjamin William Arnold

History of the Tobacco Industry in Virginia
From 1860 to 1894

ISBN/EAN: 9783337338893

Printed in Europe, USA, Canada, Australia, Japan

Cover: Foto ©ninafisch / pixelio.de

More available books at **www.hansebooks.com**

JOHNS HOPKINS UNIVERSITY STUDIES

IN

HISTORICAL AND POLITICAL SCIENCE

HERBERT B. ADAMS, Editor

History is past Politics and Politics are present History.—*Freeman*

FIFTEENTH SERIES

I-II

HISTORY OF THE TOBACCO INDUSTRY IN VIRGINIA FROM 1860 TO 1894

By B. W. ARNOLD, JR., Ph. D.

McCabe's University School, Richmond

BALTIMORE

THE JOHNS HOPKINS PRESS

PUBLISHED MONTHLY

January-February, 1897

THE FRIEDENWALD CO., PRINTERS,
BALTIMORE.

CONTENTS.

PREFACE.

The purpose of this paper is to give a fair account of the tobacco industry in Virginia since the civil war, viewing it from the standpoint both of the planter and of the manufacturer. Improvements in methods of culture, new inventions, and the technicalities of manufacture form no essential part of the subject-matter, and therefore have received but little mention. Markets, prices, distribution of profits, methods of sale and related subjects have been investigated, and these only have been treated at any length. The review has been made in an impartial spirit, and conclusions reached are based upon the historical facts presented.

Thanks are due to many manufacturers, leaf dealers and planters, for much help and valuable information, but in particular to Mr. Wm. E. Dibrell, editor of the "Southern Tobacconist and Manufacturer's Record," and Mr. J. F. Jackson, editor of the "Southern Planter," both of Richmond, Va., who have not only directed me to sources of information, but also have aided me with helpful facts and good counsel.

B. W. ARNOLD, JR.

Richmond, Va., *December*, 1896.

HISTORY OF THE TOBACCO INDUSTRY IN VIRGINIA FROM 1860 TO 1894.

INTRODUCTION.

Tobacco was first discovered by Christopher Columbus in the island of Cuba, where it grew wild, the natives smoking it either in reeds or rolled in the form of cigars. The colony of Virginia was the first to introduce the cultivation of the fragrant weed, and John Rolfe, the husband of Pochahontas, inaugurated its systematic cultivation in the colony in the year 1612. In the year 1616 Captain George Yeardly, Deputy Governor, first directed the attention of the colonists to planting it for profit, showing that its culture promised large returns, and from this time on there was an enormous and rapid increase in the annual amount grown.

The importance of tobacco to the colony of Virginia cannot well be overestimated. It was for years its currency and basis of values, the chief subject of its legislation, and the very life of its trade and commerce. In " Tobacco in Tennessee," Commissioner J. B. Killebrew has shown how its cultivation made Virginia possible; that, as a country peopled by educated, refined men and women, the state owed its existence to the plant. Tobacco has always been the chief source of Virginia's wealth, the staple product which has contributed so largely to its material prosperity. In colonial days it was the sole commodity which could be exchanged with the mother country for manufactured goods at any reasonable profit. For this reason its culture engrossed the attention of all of the colonists and entirely subordinated the remaining agricultural and manufacturing interests. In 1617, when Captain Samuel Argall arrived in the colony, as its governor, he found all the public works and buildings in Jamestown fallen to decay and not above five or six houses inhabited; the market-place, streets, and all other places planted with tobacco, and the colony dispersed, "as every man could find the properest place and the best conviency for planting."[1]   It was because tobacco was the only crop that had proved remunerative.   The search for gold had been abandoned by the colonists, and every other occupation and industry had been tried in vain. Disease, fatigue, exposure, the savage Indians, the perils of the wilderness were proving too hard for the newcomers and were rendering them hopeless and despairing.   Nothing had succeeded; nothing had paid for the making until tobacco came.   This had returned a large and rich reward for labor, and in thus bringing some promise of future wealth it had inspired the despondent colonists with new hope and encouraged them to further endeavors.   The colony began to spread and to subdue the wilderness around in spite of the savage natives and the severe labor necessitated in clearing lands.   Thus the check to decay and the stimulus to new growth and further development came from the profitableness of tobacco-growing.

A review of the colonial laws shows that tobacco gave full direction to legislation, since the majority of the statutes are only regulations concerning its culture, quality and sale. For a short while it was the source of direct revenue to the colony through a small export tax.   An effort to make it yield a revenue to sustain the postal service led to an expression of defiance to the home country anterior to the resistance of the Stamp Act by more than half a century. The low price of tobacco was one of the causes which led to Bacon's Rebellion, and it was this also which hastened the war of 1776.   The unfair dealings of the factors in England, burdening the planters with so much debt, and the heavy impositions placed upon the trade by the mother country through the system of indirect taxation, bred the

---

[1] Brock's Special Report on Tobacco for Census of 1880.

discontent which later, under the system of direct taxation, brought on the revolution.

The following table gives the growth of the trade from the year 1619 to 1775.

THE QUANTITY OF TOBACCO EXPORTED FROM VIRGINIA, AND THE PRICES, FROM 1619 TO 1775 (WITH INTERVALS), INCLUSIVE.[1]

YEAR.	CROP. Pounds.	PRICES. Per pound.	Per cwt.
1619	20,000	3*s.*	....
1620	40,000	8*d.* to 2*s.*	....
1621	55,000	....	....
1622	60,000	....	....
1628	500,000	3*s.* to 4*s.*	....
1632	....	6*d.*	....
1633	....	9*d.*	....
1639	1,500,000	3*d.*	....
1640	1,300,000	12*d.*	....
1641	1,300,000	20*d.*	....
1661	....	....	12*s.*
1662	....	....	10*s.*
1664	....	....	....
1666	....	....	....
1667	....	....	....
1682	....	....	10*s.*
1687	....	....	....
1688	18,157,000	....	....
1704	18,295,000	2*d.*	....
1729	....	2*d.*	....
1731	....	....	....
1739	....	....	12*s.* 6*d.*
1745	38,232,900	....	14*s.*
1746	36,217,800	....	....
1747	37,623,600	....	....
1748	42,104,700	....	....
1749	43,188,300	....	....
1750	43,710,300	....	....
1751	42,032,700	....	....
1752	43,542,000	....	....
1753	53,862,300	....	....
1754	45,722,700	....	....
1755	42,918,300	....	10*s.*
1756	25,606,800	....	....
1757	....	....	....
1758	22,050,000	....	50*s.*
1759	....	....	16*s.* 8*d.*
1760-1775	....	....	18*s.* to 25*s.*

[1] Brock's Special Report, Census 1880.

Since the peace of 1783 the annual exports from Virginia have not been so large. The Revolutionary War gave a check to the exportation of leaf tobacco from which it has never recovered. For 31 years immediately preceding the war the annual exports had steadily and regularly increased, but for the first 50 years after it they remained stationary, except when interrupted by wars or other commercial embarrassments. The explanation for this decrease was that the European countries, during the war, went extensively into the culture of tobacco and thereafter depended less on the western world for their supplies. The European governments had also checked the consumption of tobacco by very onerous taxation. The export trade of Virginia from the year 1800 to 1860 was as follows:

TABLE.[1]

Year.	No. Hhds.	Avg. Price per Lb.	Value.	Man'f'd. Lbs.
1800	78,686	....	....	457,713
1805	71,251	7⅜	$6,341,000	428,460
1810	84,134	5	5,048,000	529,285
1815	85,337	8	8,235,000	1,034,045
1820	83,940	8	1,188,188	593,358
1825	75,984	6⅞	5,287,976	1,871,368
1830	83,810	5½	5,833,112	3,199,151
1835	94,353	7¼	8,250,577	3,817,854
1840	119,484	6¾	9,883,657	6,787,165
1845	147,168	4¼	7,469,819	5,312,971
1850	145,729	5⅝	9,951,023	5,918,583
1855	150,213	....	14,712,468	9,624,282
1860	167,274	....	15,906,547	17,097,309

In the period since 1860 tobacco has not claimed the attention of so large a percentage of the state's population as it had hitherto. Directly after the civil war it was necessary that the farmers for several years should make food

---

[1] From a circular by John Ott, Secretary of Southern Fertilizer Company, Richmond, Va., 1876.

crops, and they were consequently more or less diverted from tobacco-growing. Freeing the slaves also necessitated the abandonment of the plantation plan of cultivating large areas. Finally in manufactures there have arisen since the war many industries which compare favorably at present with tobacco manufacture in value of output. Previous to the war the main interests of the state were agricultural, and with the exception of tobacco, iron, flour and lumber, manufactures were of comparatively little importance. These four industries engaged 46 per cent. of the state's total capital employed in manufacture; the value of their annual products was 65 per cent. of the total for the state, while the cost of their material was 74 per cent. Tobacco manufacture alone employed 31 per cent. of the hands working in factories, and furnished a product whose value was 24 per cent. of that of the whole state. Evidently general manufactures had been little encouraged and were poorly developed. The mercantile, commercial and manufacturing industries had been little sought. They did not promise that independence of position, that social distinction, wealth and leisure which the planters enjoyed who had large estates and numerous slaves to till them. Without laboring themselves, they were in a position to dispense a generous hospitality, and had the means and opportunity for storing their minds with knowledge and gaining broad and liberal culture. The mechanic, artisan, or tradesman, who had to labor with his own hands and struggle for a livelihood, was unable to do this, and consequently occupied a less honorable place in society. The depression of this useful and important class seemed to be inevitably connected with the system of negro slavery.

But after the war all this was changed. Instead of there being a preference for country life over city life, there was found a general drifting of population from the rural districts to the towns, and a tendency to engage in business, commerce and manufactures. The towns began to grow, small industries of every sort arose, and manufactures in general received much more attention. In 1860 there were only 12 manufacturing industries in Virginia which employed as much as $500,000 capital, and only 7 of these with a capital of $1,000,000; in 1890 there were 21 with a capital of $500,000, and 13 with a capital of $1,000,000.

Though tobacco is no longer the all-absorbing industry of Virginia, and its importance relative to the other industries is not so great as formerly, it still remains the chief industry of the state, the money crop of the farmers, the mainstay and support of the state's commerce. Tobacco has built and supported most of the prospering, well-established cities and towns of Virginia. Their finest residences, hotels, chambers of commerce, educational institutions and public buildings have, for the most part, been built by profits from tobacco.[1]

---

[1] Danville's growth from a population of 3,463 in 1870 to over 20,000 in 1894 was due almost entirely to the bright tobacco grown in that section. Two-thirds of the factory hands of the place are engaged in the tobacco manufactories, and about one-half of the total population are employed either in the plug factories or leaf houses. This town has paid out to tobacco planters since 1870 $79,782,312.

Lynchburg is called the " Tobacco City." Previous to 1860 the tobacco business was the only one of much importance in the place. Capital and industry sought no other channel. A citizen of Lynchburg was a tobacconist or he was nothing, and a stranger entering the town came either to buy or sell tobacco. During the seventies, however, other enterprises gained footing, and, growing rapidly, occupied to a large extent the attention of its citizens. Its tobacco trade was also injured somewhat by the establishment of many factories around it, in every part of the tobacco-growing belt formerly tributary to Lynchburg, which reduced the supply of raw material coming to this market. Notwithstanding these facts, tobacco is still the life of Lynchburg's trade, and while it has found a rival in the growth of other enterprises, it remains as ever supreme.

As to Richmond, tobacco, in the leaf trade and in manufacture, forms 25 per cent. of the city's total industry. The trade aggregates annually from eight to ten million dollars, and it employs almost as great a capital as the banks of the city. The leaf trade alone supports 120 members of the Tobacco Exchange. Here reside the " regie " purchasers for the governments of France,

Having taken this general survey of the history of the tobacco trade in Virginia, a more particular study will be made of the period from 1860 to 1894. This study naturally divides itself into two parts; the first treating of the production and sale of the leaf, the second, of the manufacture and disposal of the finished product. As the cigar industry forms but an insignificant part of the tobacco interest of Virginia, little account will be taken of it. Virginia excels in the manufacture of cigarettes, chewing and smoking, tobacco.

Italy, Spain and Austria. The exports from Richmond and Petersburg are almost exclusively of tobacco.

In 1880, of the total capital invested in the manufactures of Richmond, 28 per cent. was in tobacco manufacture; of the amount of wages paid, 35 per cent.; of value of material used, 33 per cent.; of value of product, 38 per cent. In Petersburg the percentages were still greater; of a total capital, 37 per cent. was invested in tobacco; of hands employed, 68 per cent.; of wages paid, 57 per cent.; of value of material, 72 per cent.; of value of product, 68 per cent.

PART I

PRODUCTION.

CHAPTER I.

THE RELATIVE RANK OF VIRGINIA AMONG THE TOBACCO STATES.

In 1860 Virginia produced more tobacco than any other state of the Union. The product of Kentucky, the second state of importance, was less than Virginia's by almost 16,000,000 pounds. The other principal tobacco states were Tennessee, Maryland, North Carolina, Ohio and Missouri, named in the order of precedence. Virginia raised more than three times as much as Tennessee, Maryland or North Carolina, and over four times as much as Ohio or Missouri. Her product was greater by 13,000,000 pounds than the total for the three states of Tennessee, Maryland and North Carolina. Alone she produced one-third of all the tobacco grown in the United States, and, with Kentucky, more than half. However, Virginia did not long enjoy such superiority. During the sixties, when the people were engaged in war and her fields were left untilled, the western states, and particularly Kentucky, entered extensively into tobacco-growing, and it was only a short while before the rival state had taken the place of honor. In 1870 Kentucky could boast of a production three times as large as Virginia's, and alone could claim 40 per cent. of the whole crop of the United States. Virginia still led the other states, but not at so great a distance. Ohio grew one-half as much as Virginia, and Tennessee almost three-fifths as much, while the least productive state, North Carolina, produced one-third as much as Virginia.

Since 1870 the state has held its own. Its relative position during this time is given in the following tables:

RELATIVE RANK OF ELEVEN PRINCIPAL STATES.[1]

	Acreage.			Production.			Total value.			Av. val. per acre.	
	1879, '89, '93.			1879, '89, '93.			1879, '89, '93.			1879, '89.	
Kentucky,	1	1	1	1	1	1	1	1	1	7	7
Virginia,	2	2.	2	2	2	2	2	3	2	10	8
Ohio,	6	5	5	4	3	7	5	4	8	5	5
North Carolina,	3	3	3	6	4	3	4	2	4	6	6
Tennessee,	4	4	4	5	5	4	8	6	5	11	10
Pennsylvania,	7	6	6	3	6	5	3	5	3	2	3
Wisconsin,	9	8	7	10	7	6	9	7	7	4	4
Maryland,	5	7	8	7	8	9	7	10	10	8	11
Missouri,	8	9	9	9	9	10	11	11	11	9	9
New York,	11	10	10	11	10	11	10	9	9	3	2
Connecticut.	10	11	11	8	11	8	6	8	6	1	1

STATES AND TERRITORIES.	Average value per acre. 1880–89.	Average yield per acre. 1880–89.
		Pounds.
Maine..	....	....
New Hampshire............................	....	....
Vermont....................................	....	....
Massachusetts.............................	$204 28	1485.4
Rhode Island..............................	....	....
Connecticut................................	196 58	1417.1
New York.................................	159 56	1339.6
New Jersey................................	....	....
Pennsylvania..............................	143 22	1205.3
Delaware..................................	....	....
Maryland.......	44 24	662.7
Virginia....................................	44 85	596.1
North Carolina	51 21	480.8
South Carolina............................	....	....
Georgia....................................	....	....
Florida....................................	....	....
Alabama...................................	....	....
Mississippi	....	....

[1] Compiled from the Census Reports 1880 and 1890, and U. S. Agricultural Report 1893.

STATES AND TERRITORIES.	Average value per acre. 1880-89.	Average yield per acre. 1880-89. Pounds.
Louisiana	....	....
Texas	....	....
Arkansas	50 22	578.0
Tennessee	48 30	645.4
West Virginia	56 29	609.5
Kentucky	58 63	755.2
Ohio	66 28	912.8
Michigan	64 24	503.6
Indiana	49 43	721.7
Illinois	48 18	651.9
Wisconsin	101 45	967.2
Minnesota	....	....
Iowa	....	....
Missouri	63 27	802.4
Kansas	....	....
Nebraska	....	....
California	....	....
Oregon	....	....
Nevada	....	....
Colorado	....	....
Arizona	....	....
Dakota	....	....
Idaho	....	....
Montana	...	....
New Mexico	....	....
Utah	....	....
Washington	....	....
Wyoming	....	....
Average	$61.51	727.1

CHAPTER II.

THE HISTORY OF TOBACCO PRODUCTION.

The history of production divides naturally into three periods: First, decreasing production from 1860 to 1871; second, increasing production from 1871 to 1885; third, decreasing production again from 1885 to 1894. These changes are seen in the figures of the following table, which gives Virginia's annual production from 1860 to 1894. The table is followed by explanations of the increase or decrease in the different periods.

Year.	Pounds.	Year.	Pounds.	Year.	Pounds.
1860	123,968,312	1872	48,000,000	1884	99,763,000
1861	....	1873	50,000,000	1885	107,711,000
1862	...	¹1874	35,000,000	1886	91,189,000
1863	....	1875	57,000,000	1887	79,408,000
1864	....	1876	49,000,000	1888	64,034,000
1865	....	1877	....	1889	48,522,655
1866	114,480,516	1878	89,940,000	1890	....
1867	90,000,000	1879	86,524,200	1891	....
1868	93,600,000	1880	78,421,860	1892	....
1869	65,000,000	1881	77,649,854	1893	68,599,998
1870	43,761,000	1882	89,287,332	1894	35,593,984
1871	39,384,000	1883	64,865,972		

SECTION I.—1860-1871.

The enormous decrease in these years is explained mainly by the fact that Virginia had sustained such heavy losses during the civil war. She produced little because

---

¹ The fluctuations from year to year are accounted for largely by variations in seasons, favorable or unfavorable. The year 1874 was a notably bad year for tobacco growers, only a half crop being raised. The table is prepared from Virginia and U. S. Agricultural Reports.

she was unable to produce more. Her fields were grown up in brambles and weeds; her fences, buildings and live stock were gone; her citizens were without money and with no ready means of commanding it. The planters raised all the tobacco they could, for prices were abnormally high, but they could only grow small crops, lacking capital and labor necessary for growing larger ones. They could raise in 1860 123,000,000 pounds with more ease than they could 39,000,000 pounds in 1871. The state could barely produce 36 pounds per capita in 1870, though she had produced 100 pounds per capita in 1860. She had lost productive power. In the first place her soil had been neglected and abused; secondly, her population was reduced; thirdly, her capital and credit were gone. Labor had been lost in the emancipation of the slaves; managing ability and labor in the death of soldiers, in the emigration from the state before and during the war of many foreigners who had not favored the cause of the Confederacy, and lastly, in the general drifting north and west immediately after the war of many young Virginians, who despaired of success at home under such adverse circumstances and moved out where prospects seemed brighter. Capital had been lost in the destruction of railroads and in damage to public and private property of every sort; the state had no currency and her banks were all insolvent. Her credit was lost by reason of the unsettled condition of her politics. Under these hard conditions little could be expected; agriculture was the chief industry, and this had suffered the heaviest losses; the planters were left their lands and taxes, but nothing more.

Another fact which lessened production was the inauguration of a new system of culture which was necessitated by the emancipation of the negro. The old system had been that of cultivating immense plantations with gangs of slaves, bossed by overseers, who forced the work without let or hindrance. The planter was a business manager with a large capital in land and slaves; his farms were never rented, for he found it more profitable to grow food upon them for raising negroes, since these returned from mere increase in numbers from 6 to 10 per cent. upon the capital invested. The new system was that of small farms, worked either by the owner himself, by hired labor, or by tenants on shares. The agents of production in the new order were less efficient than in the old, and, moreover, the simple readjustment of forces occasioned some friction and loss of productive power. The planter and his sons were ignorant and unskilled in methods of farming. Even the slave bosses had taken no personal part in tilling the soil, much less the wealthy planter and the young masters. The latter had spent their time in politics, self-culture, pleasure and hospitable entertainment. Tilling the soil had been the occupation of the negro heretofore, and false pride made many whites refuse to engage in it at all. Again, the negro was not as good a laborer in the new as in the old system. Many of them would work for " neither love nor money," and the labor of the few that could be persuaded to work was expensive, for overseers had to be employed to insure efficient service. The majority became so self-important in their new liberty that they refused to " hire out," but must needs rent farms on shares. They were in a position to force their claims, and the negro share-owner became a new factor in the production of the state. As he took many holidays, being a faithful attendant upon all camp-meetings, political gatherings and church festivals, he did not add much to the sum-total of the state's production.

The third cause for the decreased production was the imposition of heavy taxes upon the manufactured product. The average amount of tax on the different grades of tobacco in 1863 was 10.96 cents per pound; in 1865 it had advanced to 22.08 cents, and in 1866 it had reached the high figure of 34.77 cents. It declined a little in the next five years, but in 1871 it was still as high as 26.87 cents. The taxes on chewing and smoking tobacco, which formed the main part of Virginia's manufactures, were higher still. These ranged in 1864 from 15 to 20 cents, and in 1865 from 30 to 40 cents, according to quality. They continued as late as 1868.

The burdensome effect of these taxes upon production came through consumption. Paying 30 and 40 cents to the government on every pound of tobacco made, the manufacturer could only offer his goods at very high prices. Many who wanted tobacco were unable to buy it; the effective demand for the manufactured article was lessened, and this was reflected in a lower price for the leaf. The tax also lessened the number of buyers of leaf tobacco by restricting the manufacturing business to men of large capital. The man of small means could not pay the tax or give the necessary bond, and he had therefore to discontinue business. This meant one less buyer for the farmer's product.

Again, the manufacturers who entered the business and paid the tax were smaller buyers of leaf than they would have been without the tax. The necessity of advancing this to the government forced them to keep a part of their capital out of their business; this left them less money with which to accumulate profits, and hindered them for some years from doing business on a large scale. Thus the revival of manufacture was slower with the tax than it would have been without it, and therefore the consumption and demand for leaf were less.

Prices were also affected by the fact that only licensed dealers could buy tobacco. Previous to this the farmer could sell his product to any purchaser he might find, and frequently his market was his own tobacco barn. The agents from the factories came to the plantations and made their offers; the farmer considered the bids, and, if satisfactory, sold; if not, he left the tobacco hanging in his barn. The crop was in his own house, and no expense was incurred by allowing it to remain there. At the warehouse in the city he was forced to accept the offer of the highest bidder. It was in another man's barn, and the storage charges were steadily accumulating.

Lastly, besides the depreciation in value of the leaf, the planter had suffered still another loss. The tax had robbed him of a profit coming from the crude manufacture of the staple. Previous to the war the home industry formed no small part of the manufacture of tobacco; as the natural leaf was in strong demand, and not artificial flavorings as at present, the good old-fashioned home-made twist always found ready sale.

To summarize, the three main causes for decreased production were:

1. Virginia had been a battle-field for four years.

2. The negro had been emancipated and a new system of culture had been introduced.

3. Tobacco had been heavily taxed.

Section 2.—1871-1885.

The steady increase in these years may be partly explained by the facts that the planter had recovered in a great measure from the evil effects of the war, that he had become better acquainted with the new system of culture, and that he had learned the most profitable way of handling the freedman. In addition to these, six other causes may be mentioned which greatly favored production, viz., the lowering of the tax, the extensive use of commercial fertilizers, the introduction of improved methods of curing, the publication of much good literature on tobacco culture, the renewal and extension of the railroads, and the general development of small manufacturing towns.

In 1871 the average tax on all grades of tobacco was 26.87 cts. per pound; in 1875 it was 21.10 cts.; for the next three years it was raised to 24.24 cts., but in 1880 it was lowered again to 16 cts., and in 1884 to 8 cts. The tax on chewing and smoking tobacco was lowered in this period from 40 cts. per pound to 8 cts.

The census report of 1880 calls attention to the fact that commercial fertilizers had been very extensively employed by the tobacco planters since the year 1870. In many counties of Middle and Piedmont Virginia from 70 to 80 per cent. of the tobacco crops were fertilized with special manures, using from 150 to 300 pounds, at a cost from $3.00 to $9.00 per acre. In the tobacco counties of South-side Virginia the use of commercial fertilizers was general. From 150 to 500 pounds were employed to the acre. In 1884 there were as many as 211 different brands of commercial fertilizers sold in Virginia, and 65 of these were manufactured in that state. The large employment of manufactured manures increased production in two ways: it extended tobacco culture to poorer soils, and it increased the yield per acre.[1]

The improvements made in curing were, first, the substitution of coal for wood in firing tobacco, and afterwards the substitution of flue-curing for the process of coal-curing. This meant an economy in fuel, time and labor; less wood was required to heat the flues, less time was taken in setting the colors, and labor was no longer expended in burning the coal-pits. Moreover, the risk of burning the barns was lessened and better cures were insured, since the heat could be more easily regulated with flues than with coal or wood.

The instructive articles on tobacco published at this time increased production by educating the old planters in the best methods of culture and curing, and also by inducing

---

[1] Many soils with guano could produce a fine grade of tobacco which without it could grow none, as was the case with some sections of Henrico County, Va. The border counties of Virginia and North Carolina, covered for years with dwarf oaks, broom-sedge and pines, were reclaimed by the use of commercial fertilizers, and were converted into the choicest of lands for growing a particular variety of bright yellow tobacco. It was claimed, in the Blue Ridge district, that the yield per acre was increased from 25 to 75 per cent., and the quality from 10 to 20 per cent.; the Middle counties claimed an increase of 20 to 50 per cent., and the Southern counties, from 25 to 200 per cent.

many inexperienced farmers who had never raised tobacco to undertake the crop. Among these articles may be mentioned the helpful essays appearing in the "Southern Planter," and several papers on curing tobacco, written by Captain A. Slade, of Caswell Co., N. C. Major R. L. Ragland's famous pamphlet entitled "From the Plantbed to the Warehouse," published first in 1871, went through ten editions.

The reconstruction and extension of the railroads were made possible through the influx of northern and foreign capital. This capital began first to seek investment in Virginia in the early seventies when her interest laws were changed. On the 15th of March, 1870, the legal rate of interest was raised from 6 to 12 per cent.; it continued at this high figure until 1872, when it was lowered to 8 per cent., where it remained until 1874, when it was again lowered to 6 per cent. During these 4 years, when the law sanctioned such high returns on loans, the inflow of capital began. Another cause for this inflow was the publication of a handbook in 1868 by Commodore M. F. Maury, entitled a "Physical Survey of Virginia." The author, in making known the geography of the state, its commercial advantages, etc., showed that Virginia offered exceptional advantages for the investment of capital, and as he was a man of wide reputation, his statements won the confidence of moneyed men at home and abroad. In this way he aided greatly in procuring the large capital that was needed for restoring the old railroads to efficiency and for building the new ones needed in the full development of the state. The increase of mileage in railroads in this period was over 67 per cent.; there were 1449 miles of railroad in 1870 and 2430 miles in 1885. Most of the new roads were laid in the Valley and Appalachian portions of the state. The soil here was not favorable to tobacco, and for that reason the effect of these roads upon the state's tobacco industry was of no marked importance, though their influence upon the general trade of these sections was marvellous. They furnished new and different markets and changed both the character and direction of the trade. All they accomplished for tobacco was to extend somewhat the field of cultivation. The roads did not create any new tobacco markets nor establish small manufacturing towns; the quality of the soil forbade this. But it was quite different with the railways built on the east of the Blue Ridge in the tobacco section proper. Railroad building here consisted mainly in restoring to efficiency the old existing roads which had been torn up or gone to ruin during the war, and in laying a few local narrow-gauge branches from these out to some lumber depot, fertilizing establishment or coal mine. These roads did not change the main markets of this portion of the state, nor did they build any new large markets, for these had already been determined by the water-courses, but the roads did create and support for some years many smaller markets. Leaving the water-courses and cutting directly across the country to make shorter connections between the principal markets already established, they developed many small inland towns, which in a few years became leaf markets and active manufacturing centers.[1] Between 1870 and 1880 there were as many as 26 villages on the different roads, the tobacco trade of each of which supported one or two factories.

A final cause for increase was the fact that agriculture shared the benefits accruing from the state's newly acquired capital.

To summarize: increased production in these years was due to—

1. Recovery from the evil effects of the war.
2. A full understanding of the new system of culture.
3. Lowering of the tax.

---

[1] Bedford City, on the Norfolk & Western R. R.; South Boston, on the Richmond & Danville; Martinsville, on the Danville & New River Road; Farmville, on the Norfolk & Western; Frederick Hall, on the Chesapeake & Ohio, and Chatham, on the Virginia Midland, may be cited as such markets.

4. Use of commercial fertilizers.

5. Introduction of improved methods of curing.

6. The appearance of much good literature on tobacco culture.

7. Railroad building.

8. General development of manufacturing towns.

9. The fact that agriculture received a part of the new capital which came into the state.

SECTION 3.—1885-1894.

In this period there was a partial or entire abandonment of tobacco-growing by many of the most progressive farmers. The crop was proving less profitable than formerly. Good tobacco of medium quality which had been bringing from 12 to 25 cts. per pound was hardly wanted at prices from 6 to 15 cts. There were several causes for this decline. The village factories had disappeared, competition with the city factories having driven them from the field. The small factory began to lose its trade as soon as extensive advertising became necessary. It did not have sufficient capital for the manufacture of well-known brands, and for this reason had to give up much of its territory to larger factories and to content itself with supplying the small local trade of its own neighborhood. Since the small manufacturer had lost trade and was forced to limit his output, he was unable to run his factory regularly and to its full capacity. He could therefore no longer furnish steady employment to his whole force. When the hands were dismissed they could not find in a small village sufficient job work to support them until the factory commenced operations again, and the best of them soon left for larger places, where they could either get regular employment or have better opportunities for finding work from day to day. This meant not only loss for the village manufacturer, but also a decided gain for the city manufacturer. The latter had more and better hands to select from and could employ or dismiss them as best suited his convenience in filling orders. But following out the principle "that unto him that hath shall be given, and from him that hath not shall be taken away even that which he hath," it happened that no sooner did the village factories lessen their output (which meant a smaller consumption of leaf and lower prices) than the farmers began to ship their best tobacco to other markets which offered better prices. This left only inferior material for the village factory, while it furnished the choicest for factories located in large markets. The city factory enjoyed two other advantages: it was nearer supplies of all sorts, which saved freights; and secondly, it received special rates from the railroads on its goods, while the village factory had to pay high local rates. The discriminations in railroad charges, and indeed the railroad building of recent years, have favored the larger factories and have assisted in centralizing manufacturing interests.

Another cause for concentration and low prices in this period was the organization in the year 1890 of the American Tobacco Company, an incorporation of the leading cigarette factories north and south, which bought and sold under one management, and which had sufficient capital practically to control the prices of all cigarette tobacco, as well as the sale of all cigarette goods. The company placed a buyer in every market of importance in the state, authorizing him to buy all "cutters" suitable for its purposes and to allow no tobacco of certain classes to go to buyers for other factories except at unprofitable prices. This monopoly of "cutters" made the small markets poor ones for the agents of the large factories, who needed certain amounts of every class, and in the end it compelled the best buyers to abandon the small markets altogether. They located in the cities and made their occasional orders for leaf through the old resident manufacturer, who had already converted his factory into a warehouse or "reprizery," since his best hands and material had been lost. Thus factory life disappeared from the villages, competition was lost in the smaller leaf markets, and prices on all grades of tobacco were lowered. Ninety per cent. of the 25 villages mentioned above as having one or two factories have either closed them altogether or else do a small business for a few months in the summer, making a medium grade of chewing tobacco to sell through the country stores to farm-hands.[1]

The next explanation for lower prices, particularly of " brights," was the great extension of tobacco-growing in the states south and east, where the low price of cotton had influenced many farmers to experiment with the plant. The average value of cotton per acre in the eleven cotton-growing states for the ten years preceding 1890 had been $15.69; the average value of tobacco in the 17 tobacco states had been for the same ten years $61.51. Figures for North Carolina in the same decade showed that an acre in tobacco had brought the farmer 300 per cent. more than an acre in cotton. The southern cotton-planters saw this chance for profit and began diversifying their crops. They were encouraged and instructed by the agricultural papers and organizations within their states; the tobacco journals all over the country were filled with able articles giving explicitly and in detail the best methods of culture and curing. The fertilizer companies issued numerous pamphlets for advertising purposes which contained helpful information, while the Boards of Trade and Government Experimental Stations did all they could to encourage farmers in tobacco culture. The increase in tobacco-growing in several states is shown by the census statistics of crops for the years 1879 and 1889.

---

[1] It is true that the American Tobacco Company has placed numerous agents all through the country to buy tobacco directly from planters, and in this way has furnished new markets, but the purpose in establishing these agencies has been to avoid the competition of larger markets, and therefore prices have not been raised.

	Acres in Tobacco.	
STATES.	1879.	1889.
Florida,	90	1,190
N. Carolina,	57,208	97,077
S. Carolina,	169	394
Ohio,	34,676	44,303
Tennessee,	41,532	51,471
Kentucky,	226,120	274,587

Production was stimulated in these states, and particularly in Georgia, by the introduction of an improved method of cutting, housing and curing. The tobacco was often cured off the stalk, and not on it as formerly, the leaves being stripped as they ripened, which saved the lower leaves that before had wasted as the plant matured.[1]

But there was yet another cause for this extension south and east which probably had as much influence as all the others together, viz., Major R. L. Ragland's seed farm in Halifax County, Va. This is the largest institution of its kind in the United States. The farm had in the summer of 1895, 150,000 tobacco plants turned out for seed, representing 145 of the finest and best varieties known. The exceptional quality of the seed has influenced the largest wholesale and retail dealers to send to this farm for their supplies every year; the warehousemen, appreciating the value of select varieties, are liberal buyers, and in distributing these seeds gratuitously among their customers, extend their patronage. The Agricultural Department at Washington and consuls to foreign countries send in yearly orders to the farm for seed for distribution. When one takes into account the facts that there are 875,000 seeds to an ounce, that one-half an ounce is more than enough to insure plants for an acre, and that 75 bushels is the amount of the annual sales from this farm, one gains some idea of the influence it has had in extending production.

---

[1] Snow's Modern Barn System of Curing Tobacco.

With this extension south and east, how were prices in Virginia lowered? First, the markets of Virginia (and North Carolina) were the markets for this tobacco until enough was raised in a state to support a home market. The supply in the old markets was thus largely increased. Second, the new tobacco was mainly bright, which class had hitherto brought the fancy prices; as some of this was of first quality, it swelled the supply of this particular grade and the result was a good price, but not a. fancy one. Third, as the larger part of this new tobacco was of medium quality or nondescript—for the planters, being inexperienced, had spoiled much—when pushed into the old markets it lessened the general demand for "brights," injuring somewhat the reputation of this particular class. Fourth, since the seasons were longer in these southern states than in Virginia, their tobacco matured earlier and could be marketed before Virginia tobacco. Fifth, as the land in some of these new sections was fresher than Virginia soil, and as the farmers had adopted from the start improvements and inventions that saved labor, their tobacco was produced at less cost, and could therefore be sold at lower prices.

The last cause for a general lowering of prices in the latter part of this period (1885-1894) was the long stagnation in business due to the financial panic of 1893.

To summarize: the causes for lower prices and smaller profits in this period were—

1. Disappearance of factory life in the villages.
2. Formation of the American Tobacco Company.
3. Extension of tobacco-growing in other states.
4. Financial panic of 1893.

CHAPTER III.

There has been some specialization in the kinds of tobacco grown in Virginia. In 1860 the bulk of the tobacco produced could have been divided very fairly into two main classes.

First, the dark, heavy export tobacco, full of nicotine and creosote, cured often by air alone, but more generally by smoke and open wood fires.

Second, the red and mahogany manufacturing grades, cured in the sun or by coal fires.

These two classes are not exhaustive, for, as stated before, as early as 1850 some yellow tobacco was raised in one county of the state—Pittsylvania. However, this bright variety was not extensively produced until after the civil war. The crude methods for curing prevented a large production. Mr. John Ott, who is an authority on matters relating to tobacco, especially in Virginia and North Carolina, states that it was as late as 1856 when this type was first grown in North Carolina (by Abishia Slade). As this state had made some advance in the culture of this variety before Virginia attempted it, the assumption is fair that in 1860 this class formed but a small part of Virginia's crop. But between 1867 and 1870 it became a distinct class. Mr. Ott, in an article written in 1875, gave these types of Virginia tobacco:

A. Large, heavy, waxy, dark tobacco, esteemed so highly by European buyers.

B. Fine sun-cured mahogany, for the smoking and chewing demands of this country.

C. Bright yellow, used in adorning the plug filled with darker tobacco; also used for smoking.

He estimated that within a few years Virginia would

have a fourth type to add to her list, viz., a variety suitable for cigars. This variety has been attempted in some of the Tidewater counties, and has been grown on Ragland's seed farm in Halifax County, but has never been cultivated to any considerable extent in the state. It should not be classed with Virginia tobacco.

In the Census Report of 1880, Virginia tobacco is classified by R. L. Ragland into five distinct types, viz., 1. Dark Shippings; 2. Red and Colored Shippings; 3. Sun and Air-cured Fillers; 4. Bright Yellow Wrappers and Fillers; 5. Orange and Mahogany Flue-cured Manufacturing. These are again subdivided into as many as 18 smaller classes, e. g., the Red and Colored Shipping is divided into three classes: 1. Bright spangled; 2. Mahogany; 3. Cherry red. The Dark Shipping into 1. Dark, rich waxy, English leaf; 2. Nutmeg and Mahogany leaf, English and Continental, etc.

This classification is exhaustive and would embrace all classes produced to-day. The numerous classes are not to be understood, however, as so many new varieties introduced between 1875 and 1880. The five main heads are more or less included in the three classes first mentioned. The idea to be conveyed by the comparison of these classifications is simply that there has been more and more specialization in tobacco production. Some new, distinct varieties have been introduced, but for the most part the types are the same, only differently handled to meet special needs of certain markets.

SECTION 2.—CHANGES IN DEMAND.

During the years immediately preceding the war, the markets both in the United States and foreign countries handled chiefly dark tobaccos. The "brights" had not been produced long enough, nor in sufficient abundance, to give the home and foreign markets full acquaintance with them. The domestic trade had not as yet fully appreciated their good qualities, and the export trade had had no opportunity to learn them. The French, who were fastidious in taste and epicures in everything, had already shown a preference for milder grades of tobacco, and had been getting for some years a piebald grade, which, though cured with open wood fires, was so slowly cured that it was made yellower than the average export grade, and was not so strong with nicotine and smoke. But this was not at all like the bright yellow tobacco which Virginia and North Carolina began to produce in a small way immediately before the war, when the process of coal-curing was introduced, and so abundantly after it, when the process of flue-curing was perfected. The small amount of bright tobacco grown at this time was all used at home, and even here its advantages for manufacturing purposes were not widely known. The factories still demanded the rich dark grades; sweet sun-cured, wine-colored fillers, and waxy, mahogany wrappers.

But in the seventies, ten or fifteen years after this, the bright tobaccos were in full demand all over the United States. The change had come about in this way. While Virginia and North Carolina were engaged in war, and their factories and trade were stopped for so many years, other states, and notably the western ones, Kentucky, Ohio and Missouri, entered entensively into the cultivation and manufacture of tobacco. Since heavy taxes had been laid and much capital was needed to enter this business, these states, which had suffered little from war, were able to do business on a much larger scale than the southern states, whose losses were so serious. They began in 1874 a big system of advertisement, which put the Virginia factories at a great disadvantage; the latter were unaccustomed to this method of sale, and they were also unable to adopt it extensively. Virginia had been in the habit of selling, on its merits alone, about one-third of all of the manufactured tobacco used in the United States, and naturally felt that this long established reputation would continue its sale. The manufacturers were slow to advertise even as much as they could. The results were that the Virginia tobaccos were not kept before the public, while the western brands were, and that the public, being unable to procure the former, acquired a taste for the latter.

The new western tobacco was very different from the Virginia type. The plug was a soft, cheesy, sweet one, made from a variety of leaf called the White Burley, which had proved especially suited to the grassy soils of the western states, and which has since enjoyed an unrivalled reputation as a filler. The main quality which recommended it so highly for manufacturing purposes was its absorptive power. Being a tough, spongy, porous leaf, it would absorb flavoring to the amount of 25 to 40 per cent. of its own weight; the Virginia leaf had little absorptive power, and would funk and damage if too much sweetening material was put upon it. The western filler was also cheaper; the cost of production was less where fresh grass lands were used than where old worn-out soil was employed or where timber lands had to be cleared. Moreover, the process of air-curing employed with the Burley leaf was less expensive than that of flue or coal-curing. Another advantageous quality was its mildness; it made a popular chew. With these points in its favor, it was natural that the western filler should be largely substituted for the Virginia filler. In the year 1881 the " Southern Planter " wrote as follows concerning this change: " The White Burley produced in the west has now thoroughly substituted our dark grades, both for manufacturing and shipping, so much that few men in the trade have the courage to deal in either. Many plug manufacturers never go into the Tobacco Exchange (Richmond), and one shipper receives from an English correspondent an order to send no more Virginia leaf, as the White Burley now rules the roost." The Richmond manufacturers were using at this time about five times as much Burley as Virginia leaf.

This full substitution of western tobacco naturally resulted in a smaller demand for the average Virginia filler, but it increased the demand for another grade, viz., the bright yellow type, which was being produced extensively at this time in the counties bordering on the North Carolina line. A fine golden wrapper was wanted to put around the plug formed of the Burley filler to beautify it; a combination of the Virginia bright leaf and the western mild leaf promised to meet popular demand and to make wide sales. The bright plug was introduced, and for ten years it ruled the market and was the rage and fashion of the domestic trade.

Another potent influence in increasing the demand for bright tobacco in these years was the development of cigarette manufacture. This business was introduced to the world at the Exposition in Philadelphia in 1876 by John F. Allen & Co., of Richmond, Va., who made at that time a very creditable exhibit of their goods. They were not then at all aware, however, of the great future of cigarettes, for fine plug, fine cut and smoking tobaccos were their leading brands, and cigarettes were only packed for the trade in order to sell those brands. But no sooner were the new goods presented to the public than there arose a large and ever-increasing demand for them, and cigarette machines being invented soon after this, the business grew marvellously, far beyond the expectation of the firm which had introduced them.[1]

Another effect of the cigarette exhibit at the Exposition

---

[1] The profitableness of the business will be seen from this short paragraph, appearing in the " Southern Tobacconist and Manufacturer's Record " for 1892, headed " Cigarette Millionaires." " Major Lewis Ginter's total wealth is valued now at $13,000,000; he made every cent of this in cigarettes. He might have been worth one-fourth as much more, for he had the habit of giving this much of his income regularly to charity. Mr. Francis Kinney is worth $10,000,000; George Arents, Maj. Ginter's nephew, is worth $3,000,000; John Pope, Ginter's partner, is worth $2,000,000. Mr. Wm. Marbury, Mr. P. Whitlock, Mr. Wm. S. Kimball, Mr. Butler of the Kinney Branch, Mr. Emery of Goodwin Branch, each have a million and over."

was to increase the demand for bright tobacco abroad. The foreigner had gotten at this time his first taste of Virginia bright leaf and he preferred it to the Turkish yellow leaf which had been his only dependence hitherto for smoking purposes. The foreign demand was stimulated also by the publications of Mr. John Ott, who had collected many favorable data on bright tobacco and had spread the information broadcast in pamphlet form all over England and America. He wrote concerning the foreign demand in 1876, " In observing the tendency of the trade, we find quite a demand is setting in from Europe for our ' sun-cured ' and ' fancy brights,' besides the usual call for what good heavy shipping we have to offer. Germany is taking with reasonable freedom sun-cured lugs, and England a great deal of bright yellow leaf." This year marks the beginning of the bright export trade. Since that time Canada, Austria, England and France have all been giving annually larger orders for Virginia brights at prices varying from 6 to 15 cents per pound.

Changes in demand in the period of the nineties remain to be considered. We find that fashion as to plug tobacco has undergone a decided change. The golden wrapper which formed almost 12 to 15 per cent. of the cost of the plug had proved in many instances deceptive. As a fifty-cent wrapper might contain within it a four- or five-cent quality of filler, it was misleading, making a poor piece of tobacco appear as well as a good piece. Lacking also good chewing qualities, it was frequently pulled off the plug and thrown away. The bright plug ceased to be much in demand. A rich mahogany wrapper of fine texture and good chewing qualities was called for, and the gold tobacco was allowed to pile up on the shelves of the retail merchants for want of buyers. As the mahogany wrappers were more abundant than the yellow wrappers, the leading factories adopted them for their chief brands, and by means of extensive advertising they greatly assisted in determining the new character of the trade. To compete with these large factories, having popular and well established brands, it was necessary for smaller ones to employ the same wrappers on their goods; and soon all the manufacturers ceased to offer fabulous prices for the white wrappers, but relegated them to a place with cutters and granulated stock, which commanded lower prices.

The demand for cigarette tobacoo also experienced a change, caused by the formation of the American Tobacco Company. The company exercised two effects upon the bright tobacco market, one of which was creditable, the other was not. In the company's favor it can be said that by its large system of extensive advertisement throughout the United States and in foreign countries, which it has been able to carry out by reason of its enormous capital and profits, it built up a market for cigarettes that could not possibly have been gained by the individual competitive factories, working independently of each other. This ever widening market sustained, in spite of great over-production, fair prices all the while on the particular cutter grades. To the company's discredit it can be said that it materially lowered the price to the producer on all grades of bright tobacco.

Reviewing the export trade in the nineties, we note two new changes; first, the annual exportations were steadily decreasing from year to year; and secondly, bright tobacco was forming a much larger proportion of these exports. More "brights" were going abroad now because they had fallen considerably in value, the foreign demand varying inversely as the price. The decrease in total exports was due to two causes: first, the cheapness of certain grades of tobacco in the West as compared with prices in Virginia; second, the contract system of buying employed by the "regie" monopolies.

The first cause explains why Germany imported only one-third as much of Virginia tobacco at this time as it had done ten years before, and since Bremen is the chief open market of the Continent, the decrease in Germany's imports represented fairly the decrease in the imports of Europe.

France, Italy, Austria and Spain have "regie" monopolies; that is to say, their tobacco industry is under the supervision and control of the government, and their leaf dealers, manufacturers, retailers, etc., are appointees of the government. All these countries, except Austria,[1] have adopted the plan of giving their orders for Virginia tobacco by type samples to those who promise to supply them at the lowest figures. This system has injured Virginia's trade in two ways; first, orders have been taken at such low figures that the buyers could not get Virginia tobacco at these prices and they have been forced to go west to fill their orders; second, the low bids have forced the buyers to fill their orders with the meanest grades of western tobacco, and this vile stuff has been shipped back to the different governments under the name of Virginia tobacco, and has thus greatly injured its reputation abroad.[2]

The following statistics of Virginia's foreign shipments

---

[1] Austria, however, though having a government monopoly in tobacco, is not subject to the same censure, for it has pursued quite a different plan in purchasing its supplies. This country buys its tobacco through its consul, who resides in Virginia, and who can see that it is to the interest of Austria, as well as Virginia, to maintain reasonable prices. The long, broad, dark wrappers, suitable for making the Austrian cigars, and grown best in certain counties of Virginia, are always in strong demand at from 11 to 16 cents.

[2] The contract system employed in these foreign countries has been introduced since the war, and of late years it has materially lowered the prices offered by them for tobacco, and has, consequently, greatly decreased the amount of Virginia's exports. In the sixties France paid as high as 12 and 15 cents for her tobacco, and imported from Virginia annually about 8000 hogsheads; Italy paid 12 to 16 cents, and imported 4000 hogsheads; Spain paid 8 to 10 cents, and imported 2500 hogsheads. At present France pays 5 and 6 cents, and imports 1200 hogsheads; Italy pays from 8 to 12 cents, and imports about 1500 hogsheads. Spain gives such low prices, 3 and 4 cents, that it can practically get no Virginia tobacco whatever; it imports about 12,000 to 20,000 hogsheads of the commonest western tobacco to be found.

show how much her exports have decreased in the past
ten years.[1]

Year.	Hhds. Tobacco.	Hhds. Stems.
1884–85	23,070	2,802
1885–86	28,700	3,218
1886–87	21,376	2,812
1887–88	22,063	2,647
1888–89	19,230	1,369
1889–90	21,417	1,731
1890–91	19,829	1,465
1891–92	19,705	1,631
1892–93	14,676	1,375
1893–94	15,212	1,116

[1] New York Custom House.

CHAPTER IV.

THE PLANTER.

The most important and interesting facts in connection with the planter may be brought out in answering the following five enquiries:

1. What has he considered burdens upon agriculture in general, and upon tobacco culture in particular?
2. What has he done to remove these burdens?
3. What has been his explanation of the general decline in prices?
4. Does he study the wants of his market?
5. To what extent has the price of tobacco made him restrict acreage and diversify crops?

Section 1.—What has the planter considered burdens upon agriculture in general, and upon tobacco culture in particular?

A review of the agricultural papers of the state shows that the farmers as a class have considered the following things burdensome: 1. Unequal and unnecessary taxation. 2. Contracted currency. 3. Discriminating charges of railroads. 4. Trusts. 5. Trade exactions. 6. An over-supply of middlemen. They maintain that unequal taxation has arisen, first, from high protective tariffs, which have favored the manufacturing industries of the country and made abnormally high prices for manufactured goods, but left agricultural products unprotected. Secondly, they maintain that the farmer's property, being largely in land, farm stock and implements, is incapable of concealment, unlike money, bonds, stocks, and that therefore all his possessions are listed for taxation, while much more productive capital in other forms is totally exempt. The large accumulation of money in the United States Treasury in the year 1889 was considered sufficient proof that taxation had been unnecessarily heavy. The government was declared guilty of cheapening the price of products of the field by contracting the currency, taking it out of the pockets of the people and out of circulation without necessity. This contraction of currency was believed by many farmers to be the underlying cause of their troubles. Give them free coinage of silver, more money, they argued, and their grievances would end. Their faith in the white metal was as unbounded as many of their arguments in support of its free coinage were groundless and unsound. The majority of Virginia farmers are " silverites," but contrary to the general impression on this subject, there are many among them who favor only the yellow metal. The chief agricultural paper of the state [1] has always firmly held to the single gold standard, and its able support of that side of the question has made some monometallists among the planters.

The agricultural papers are full of accounts of discriminating rates and exorbitant charges by railroads. By means of the table of transportation rates in the report of the United States Agricultural Department for June, 1890, an interesting comparison was made between the rates in Virginia and those of other states. Rates on agricultural implements to New York City from Erie were 18 cts. per cwt.; from Cleveland, 21½ cts.; from Detroit, 22½ cts.; from Cincinnati, 26 cts.; from Chicago, 30 cts.; and the rates on carloads of sheep from all these places to New York were about 2 cts. lower still per cwt. In Virginia the rates of transportation from Richmond to South Hill, a distance of about 90 miles on the Atlantic & Danville R. R., were on groceries 17 cts. per cwt. and on first-class goods 55 cts.; on sheep in crates they were $1.75 per cwt. gross.

The rates have been made to favor long hauls as against short ones, or in other words, the manufacturer and the dealer have been favored in being allowed cut rates, while the producers have been compelled to pay full charges.

---

[1] " Southern Planter," of Richmond, Va.

Nothing need be said of trusts. The intense hatred of the farmers for combinations of all sorts is well known. They believe that " combines " have no redeeming features whatever, and curiously many have begun to regard industrial organizations of all kinds among town people as partaking more or less of the nature of trusts. All organizations of merchants, boards of trade, bankers' associations and incorporated stock companies are considered by many farmers to be trusts whose purpose is to oppress. According to this reasoning they should apply the same opprobrious name to their own clubs and agricultural societies.

By trade exactions the farmers mean excessive charges by warehousemen for small services rendered. They claim that the warehousemen act as factors and not as commission merchants, that they speculate on the farmer's produce, buying it themselves and selling at a profit rather than seeking to get the highest price for the farmer.

The middlemen, according to the majority of the farmers, are the factors, brokers, commission merchants, canvassers, dealers, drummers, peddlers, pin-hookers, speculators, sharpers, traders, etc. The farmers claim that these men are more numerous than necessary; that the same amount of work could be done by a smaller number of men, and that they have the unnecessary ones to support.

Of the six evils to agriculture named above, four are considered to rest with peculiar weight upon tobacco culture, viz., taxation, trusts, trade exactions and middlemen. The farmers say that the tax has been a double one on them, that they have paid it first in the fall of price of the leaf and again in purchasing the manufactured product. The tax lowered the price of leaf in three ways: first, it limited consumption; second, it only allowed licensed dealers to purchase tobacco; third, when the tax was very heavy it placed the manufacturer's main chance for profit in the reduction of the price of leaf. Since the other costs, of labor, material and tax were all fixed in amount, a wider sale of the manufactured product could only be had by reducing the price, which could only come through a reduction in price of the leaf, since this was the only variable element in the composite price for the finished product.

The combination that most actively arouses the antagonism of the planter is the American Tobacco Company. One has but to mention the word combine or monopoly to a farmer to bring forth burning maledictions against this company. He believes that this one organization has done more to lower prices and to make tobacco-growing unprofitable than all other causes combined. But another form of union to which he points as having greatly lessened competition in the medium-sized markets is that of concerted action on the part of the tobacconists and bankers, a mutual understanding among them to guard well each other's interests. It is said, and it is true, that most of the large tobacco dealers, or factory owners, in a town are large stockholders in the banks. It is claimed that if these men expect to need a large amount of money to make special purchases they instruct the men in the banks to let no small amounts go out until they are first accommodated. Many of the buyers on these markets are men of small means, speculators, who borrow small sums from the banks for a few days, enter the market and make things lively trying to turn over their money. Since these small buyers cannot get accommodation at the bank, they are unable to make purchases—the business being conducted on a cash basis—and therefore the number of buyers in these small markets is lessened, prices fall, and the market awaits the pleasure of the moneyed stockholders.

As to the trade exactions complained of, the warehouse charges, they assert that these have been much higher under the system of private inspection and private warehouses than they were just after the war under the system of state inspection and public warehouses. Most of the tobacco was then sold in hogsheads, under the supervision of the state, samplers being appointed by the Governor. Inspection was necessary to insure the buyer, as tobacco was often nested, common tobacco being hid inside the good, and sometimes trash, such as stones or sticks, put inside of this.　The bulk of Virginia's tobacco was exported at that time, and without inspection its reputation could not have been maintained abroad.　But when bright tobacco began to flood the markets, which was sold for the most part on the warehouse floor, not packed in hogsheads, but scattered in small piles, where the buyer could examine easily for himself the quality of the tobacco, inspection was no longer necessary.　Accordingly, in the year 1874 a change was made in the laws which allowed all loose tobacco to be sold without governmental inspection.　Three years later state inspection was abolished altogether, and the trade was given the right to elect its own inspectors and to make its own charges.　The farmers claim that these charges are higher than formerly.[1]

---

[1] The following comparison of charges under the old and new system is taken from the " Progressive Farmer ":

" Let us contrast the sales of 10 hogsheads of tobacco sold under the *old regime* and under prices *now* (1889) charged by the warehousemen generally.

OLD CHARGES.

Inspection and warehouse charges on 10 hhds. tobacco
at $1.45 per hhd. ....$ 14.50
Commission charge selling 10 hhds. at $1.00 each......　10.00

Full charge paid by planter.........................$ 24.50
Paid to the State 30 cts. per hhd. on 10 hhds..........　3.00

Leaving to inspectors ....$ 21.50

PRESENT CHARGES.

Weighing 15,000 pounds at 10 cents per 100 pounds....$ 15.00
Auction fees, say on 50 piles at 25 cents each..........　12.50
Commission on 15,000 pounds sold at 10 cents per pound
—$15.00 or 2½ per cent.............................　37.50

$ 65.00

Showing that warehousemen now charge *over three times* as much as was formerly paid inspectors for like service when sold in hhds.

LOOSE TOBACCO.

Old charges on fifteen thousand pounds...............$ 24.00
Present warehouse charges ....　65.00"

Section 2.—What has the planter done to remove his burdens?

For the most part he has talked and done nothing. He has envied the well-to-do and abused those in authority whom he considered responsible for the oppressive laws. At times, however, he has attempted more and with varying degrees of success. He has believed that unjust laws were his burdens, that relief from them could come only through the legislature, and therefore he has directed his efforts towards influencing the actions of this body. The earliest attempt of the farmers within our period of study to shape legislation was in the year 1866, when they were suffering so much for the want of capital and labor. In November of that year there assembled in Richmond a body of agriculturalists called " The Virginia State Agricultural Society of Virginia Farmers." The object of the meeting was to advise as to the best methods to pursue in agriculture under the new and harsh conditions which the war had imposed; to discuss the relative merits of the slave system and hired labor; and finally to devise some means of getting more labor and money with which to cultivate their lands. Committees were appointed who returned full reports to the convention for its consideration and endorsement. The one on usury laws submitted a resolution which advised the legislature to repeal the existing laws, which only allowed a maximum rate of 6 per cent. interest, and to enact a law which, while leaving 6 per cent. as the legal rate, should also declare that contracts for any higher rate whatever should be valid, provided they had been made in writing. A bill to this effect was drafted by the convention and presented to the legislature. It failed of passage at the time, but in 1870 a similar bill became a law, showing that the farmers' demand had not been altogether unheeded. The legal maximum rate of interest was raised from 6 to 12 per cent. The resolution of the Labor Committee, sent to the legislature, advised that body to encourage immigration, and to that end to make necessary appropriations. This was not without effect, for later a Board of Immigration was formed, under whose supervision were issued many pamphlets and handbooks presenting the resources and natural advantages of Virginia and aiding greatly in bringing people and money into the state.

In the year 1874, when the trade of Richmond endeavored to abolish the state inspection laws, the farmers brought very strong and effective influence to bear upon the legislature. The planters desired the retention of state inspection under sworn bonded inspectors, appointed by the Governor, and charges regulated by law. They feared to surrender to the trade the appointment of private inspectors under rules, regulations and charges of the so-called tobacco exchanges, which they believed were always ready and anxious to take undue advantage. To meet the organized trade they decided to organize themselves; and fifteen counties in the heart of the tobacco-growing district of the state began holding public meetings, in which the action of the Richmond trade was denounced as a deliberate attempt to rob the planter of his natural rights, and resolution after resolution was drafted petitioning the lawmakers in Richmond to retain at all hazards the old inspection laws. A few able representatives were persuaded to take the planter's side in the contest and the result was a victory for the farmers. State inspection was then retained, although later, in the legislature of 1877-1878, these laws were changed. As to the tobacco tax, the legislature has always been on the side of the farmers, trying constantly to persuade congress to reduce it further. The planter has fought the tax from the first, and has forced reduction as far as he could by denouncing the iniquitous exaction through the papers and by returning to the legislature those members who worked hardest for the reduction. To rid themselves of high tariffs they have regularly voted the Democratic ticket; to get relief from trade exactions, railroad discriminations and middlemen they have worked through the organization of the Farmers' Alliance.

This order first entered the state in the year 1887. By the year 1891 it had formed Alliances in 96 different counties, had started 20 County Alliance stores, had established five district exchanges, each with a capital stock of $2,000, and had gained the large membership of 35,000. Its purpose at first seemed a strictly business one, and as a business organization it prospered and proved very helpful to its members. Later its whole purpose seemed political, and as a political body it has not been successful. With business ends in view it had endeavored to establish closer relations between the agriculturists on the one hand and the merchants and manufacturers on the other, to give the farmers the benefit of buying goods in large quantities and to save them the profits of many unnecessary middlemen. Farm supplies and various manufactured goods could be bought in the Alliance stores at factory prices plus the freight, which generally saved them 25 per cent. on their purchases. The district exchanges in the larger cities saved them from 30 to 40 per cent. on farm implements, fertilizers, salt, etc. The Alliance fertilizer factory near Richmond, capitalized at $5,000, reduced the price on most brands of fertilizer sold in Virginia at least 25 per cent.

To save themselves from heavy warehouse charges, the Alliance built several warehouses and undertook to run them at lower rates than were generally charged. They opened with fair promise, but soon found that the patronage was not sufficient to justify the reduction made in rates and were forced to raise them or close. This shows that the evil of excessive warehouse charges was imaginary and not real; competition having made the charges as low as would support the business.

In the year 1891 the Farmers' Alliance went into politics and gained a large representation in the General Assembly. The Alliance representation in the Senate at this time was one-fourth of its membership, and in the House of Delegates one-half. The Alliance men in the General Assembly outnumbered either of the old parties, Democrat as well as Republican, and in the lower house the party was as strong as the Democrats and Republicans combined. The farmers held at last the long-coveted power of making laws, and they determined to enact a number sufficient to save themselves from all present embarrassments and to provide against all future contingencies. Their railroad bill was an interesting one, though drastic, far-reaching and impracticable, as were also some of the other measures proposed against trusts and national banks. These bills embraced such wide and varied interests that no body of sensible men could be persuaded to pass them until their full effects had been well weighed and duly considered. Free discussion of the bills brought out their imperfections and made many of the most loyal Alliance members vote against them. The forces divided, the minority gained the balance of power and none of their proposed bills became laws. The few really practical bills introduced, those dealing with fertilizers, seeds, cattle diseases, etc., which would have proved of material benefit to the farmer, received only the smallest share of attention. The farmers would not consider bills so small in their requirements; they must needs make great laws or none. With the power in their own hands they were unable to use it to advantage.

Section 3.—The explanation given by the planters for general decline in prices.

All planters agree that there has been a gradual fall in the price of tobacco since the war, but they differ as to the amount of the fall and as to its causes. A few hold that tobacco has maintained a higher price than any other farm product; that the prices of all products have declined by reason of the steadily contracting volume of the currency, but that the price on tobacco has been lowered less than that of any other product by reason of the ever increasing demand for it. They claim, too, that the farmers do not bring as good a quality of tobacco to the markets now as formerly; that present prices of inferior have been compared with past prices of good tobacco, and that in this way prices have seemed to decline. They admit that prices fluctuate a good deal, that in particular years the general prices have been low, and that of late years the prices on certain grades have been lower than ever before, but they attribute the fall in prices to over-production, to bad seasons, bad management, and not to burdensome laws, combines, trade exactions, etc., which they consider only minor causes. Taking for example the year 1878, when prices on all grades were exceedingly low, the average price in the United States being 5 cents, and in Virginia only 4.8 cents; they calculate the stocks on hand in the principal markets of the world, viz., London, Liverpool, Bremen, New Orleans, Baltimore and New York, and find that the increase in stocks in the year 1878 over that of 1875 was 70,115 hogsheads, and that all this was of very inferior quality. Reviewing next the report of the Agricultural Department, they see that the four years immediately preceding 1878 were those of enormous increase in production all over the United States, and that since the year 1874, when hardly half a crop was grown on account of extremely bad seasons, and when prices were abnormally high by reason of the small supply on hand, the farmers had been planting more and more every year until they finally glutted the market in 1877. As conclusive proof that over-production was the main cause of low prices at this time, and not, as some claimed, the agitation of the tax, or the general stagnation in business due to the panic of '73, they give the figures of production in those years, which certainly strengthen their statements.

For United States.		Price.
1874	178,355,000 lbs.	13.1
1875	379,347,000 "	8.
1876	381,002,000 "	7.4
1877	581,500,000 "	5. (?)

Ten years later, in 1886 and 1887, prices were again very low, and especially on all medium grades of both dark and bright tobacco. One explanation given by them was that the farmer had become daft in regard to curing all his tobacco yellow, that he had attempted to flue-cure for " brights " when his tobacco had not yellowed well on the hill; another was that the farmer had used land unsuited to the type and had without reason followed the general maxim of "the lower the price, the larger the crop."

These explanations of prices are accepted by a few well-to-do, progressive farmers who own large, well-kept estates and who have money enough for their own farms and also for small investments in the towns and cities. They are not at all satisfactory, however, to the great majority of farmers, who either possess only a few acres, or else are tenants, raising crops on shares. Having worked hard to raise the finest tobacco possible and having received every year less and less money for the same quality, they claim, first, that tobacco has suffered a reduction in price not only common to all farm products, but one peculiar to itself, and secondly, that this reduction is due not to the farmer or any of his methods, but to causes which at present are entirely beyond his control.

To prove the first point they give accounts of actual sales in different years. A farmer from Louisa County, who is a skilled hand in tobacco culture, brought to the Richmond market in 1877 a crop of sun-cured tobacco raised on three acres of land, for which he received for his best grades from 25 to 43 cents per pound and for his lowest grades from 8 to 15 cents per pound. In 1895 he carried to the same market a crop of the same size, same quality, raised by the same hands and on the same soil, the land in the meantime greatly improved. Tobacco was low, but by reason of the good quality of this lot he expected to realize on his highest grade from 10 to 15 cents per pound and for the lowest from 5 to 8 cents. What he did receive was for the highest from 7 to 9 cents, and for his lowest from 4 to 6 cents. Another expert farmer from the same county averaged in 1888 12½ cents per pound all around, and in 1892 for the same grades only 9 cents average. Bright wrappers some years after the war sold from 50 to 70 cents, and some brought as much as $1.50 to $2 per pound. They now range from 12 to 40 cents and seldom go so high as 50 or 60 cents. Cutters brought in 1885 from 15 to 30 cents; they now bring only 8 to 22 cents. The quotations of the bright tobacco market of Danville are indicative of the fall in prices. For the three years of 1883, '84 and '85 the average price on all grades was 13.3 cents, while for 1892, '93 and '94 it was only 7.8 cents. Such facts as these afford proof enough to the majority of farmers that prices of tobacco have suffered an enormous decline in the last few years. Their reasons for it would be the formation of the American Tobacco Company, the small combinations among agents buying for different factories, and the fact that the large manufacturers own much stock in the banks. They would admit, too, that over-production had in some degree affected prices, but they have no patience with the theory which lays all blame at the farmer's door.

Section 4.—Does the planter study the wants of his market?

The average planter makes very little effort to learn the demands of his market. As one knows him better, he becomes more and more convinced of this lamentable fact. The farmer rarely reads a newspaper, seldom goes ten miles from home, and consequently has to depend almost entirely on hearsay for a knowledge of his market. He is so constantly employed with his farm duties that he can spare no time in finding whether or not he is making a salable product. He sees his market once a year, the day on which he sells his crop, and judges of its future requirements by its present wants. He never visits other markets nor reads reports of them, and consequently his idea of the actual demands of the general tobacco market

is exceedingly vague. If he is willing to adapt his production to varying demands, his imperfect knowledge will
frequently lead him to make improper changes. When he
is not guided by custom he is misled by ignorance. The
tobacco journals generally note any decided changes occur-
ring in the markets' wants and advise wisely as to the best
grades to raise, but the farmers as a class do not read the
journals. A small minority of the planters in the state,
however, act more rationally. Some of these are Virginia
farmers bred and born, but a number of them are immi-
grants from the north and west who have recently moved
to the state. By farming on business principles, studying
first their markets and then furnishing them with suitable
supplies, they have succeeded where others have failed.

An able lawyer of Amelia Court House gives this case
of successful farming which has come under his own obser-
vation: Ten years ago, he said, the land in Amelia County,
five miles south of Amelia Court House, was delinquent
for taxes. The farmers cultivating it were getting poorer
and poorer every year. Some Pennsylvania farmers
moved in, bought the land, and after a little improvement
and manuring began to grow a particular grade of export
tobacco called the Austrian Wrapper, used in Austria for
cigars. This grade brings from 12 to 15 cents per pound.
To-day these farmers have paid for their lands, put them in
fine condition, built good houses, and their prospects are
fine for becoming rich farmers. None of their lands can
be bought or rented now for reasonable sums since they
have proved so profitable in the hands of their owners.
Another planter of the same county who specialized on a
heavy dark export grade, employing the intensive system
of cultivation, reported as follows: " I planted 17 acres in
tobacco on my farm in the year 1892, on which I used
about 6½ tons of fertilizer. I raised on these 17 acres
and sold in the Richmond market about 25,750 pounds for
$3,006.42, less freight and commission. In the year 1890
I raised on about 17½ acres upwards of 27,000 pounds

and sold it for $2,400." A Halifax County planter, who had specialized on a grade of bright tobacco, writes that he netted in 1895 $6,500 on 22 acres, which is an average of $282.46 to the acre.

Such have been the profits for a few planters who have specialized in their production and succeeded in meeting profitably the market's demands. The Commissioner of Agriculture states that in those counties where there is most specialization in production and diversification of crops (Piedmont, Tidewater and Valley), the farmers have a large number of clubs, are more regular in their attendance on the Farmers' Institutes, and take more agricultural papers. The editor of the " Southern Planter " of Richmond states that immigrant farmers as a rule take one or two agricultural papers. This may explain in a measure their success. This taste or desire for reading is wanting in the Virginia farmer, and must be cultivated if he is to compete successfully with those who farm on scientific principles.

Section 5.—To what extent have the low prices of tobacco made farmers restrict acreage and diversify crops?

Virginia planters are not raising at present as much tobacco as they did 8 or 10 years ago. The low price of the staple product has compelled a diversification of crops in many localities with intensified farming for the old crops, and with extensive farming for pasturage, stock raising, etc. In the Piedmont counties fruits have been substituted for tobacco; in parts of Middle Virginia, grain, hay and stocks; in the Tidewater counties, trucks and vegetables. In the report of the Commissioner of Agriculture for 1888 there were only 23 counties which reported tobacco as the main money crop, while there were 53 which reported grain; 11, trucks; 4, fruits, and 4, peanuts. Ten years before this at least 30 would have reported tobacco as their chief dependence for money. Several mountain counties in the western part of the state, Giles, Craig and Greene, which six or seven years ago were large producers of tobacco, have of recent years grown none whatever.

The land here being very hilly and steep, was washed into gullies soon after clearing, and as the fertilizer went with the loam of the soil to the low lands at every freshet, the soil was soon rendered unfit for tobacco and the crop had to be abandoned. In the year 1888, out of 18 counties reporting, 16 declared an increase in the raising of horses, 9 in cattle, 13 in poultry for market, 12 in garden vegetables. The restriction of acreage in the last four years for 16 main tobacco counties is represented in the table given below.[1]

---

[1] Per cent. of acreage planted in tobacco in 16 tobacco counties of Virginia for the four years, 1891-1894:

COUNTIES.	1894.	1893.	1892.	1891.
Louisa	75	87	...	100
Caroline	62	100	100	...
Fluvanna	78	95	100	100
Franklin	65	76	75	85
Floyd	67	89	100	96
Appomattox	87	100	...	100
Cumberland	67	90	...	100
Bedford	62	99	110	105
Botetourt	..	80	...	100
Campbell	70	90	...	105
Charlotte	78	90	100	88
Lunenburg	.88	90	90	90
Mecklenburg	70	97	100	110
Pittsylvania	70	90	80	83
Henry	65	81	100	100
Halifax	60	100	90	96

From reports of Commissioner of Agriculture in Virginia.

PART II

MANUFACTURE.

CHAPTER V.

THE RELATIVE RANK OF VIRGINIA AMONG THE TOBACCO STATES.

"To the state of Virginia the commercial world is indebted for the rise and progress of the tobacco trade, and to Virginia manufacturers the trade owes whatever of good there is to be found in the manifold improvements that have been made in the form and quality of the various brands embraced under the general name of plug tobacco." Such was the tribute paid to Virginia in the early sixties by J. L. Bishop in his "History of American Manufactures." The state manufactured at this time 75 per cent. of the total product made in the United States. Until the last ten years she led all the states in the amount of plug tobacco made, and prior to 1881 she stood first in the total amount of all manufactured tobacco products; a few years after this she was overtaken and outstripped by Missouri. In the year 1880 Virginia manufactured more tobacco than the three states of New York, New Jersey and Pennsylvania together, or the four states of Kentucky, Missouri, Arkansas and Tennessee, or the eight states of Indiana, Illinois, Ohio, Michigan, Wisconsin, Iowa, Kansas and Nebraska. Virginia had the same precedence in the matter of revenue paid. The state manufactured more than twice as much as both Maryland and North Carolina and paid more than twice the revenue of these two states. Virginia's contribution to the total revenue of the United States from all sources was in 1880 13.8 per cent., and to the revenue from plug, smoking and fine-cut it was 24½ per cent.; in 1893 her contributions were only 8 per cent. and 11⅔ per cent. respectively. In the manufacture of cigarettes the state has always maintained a prominent position. In 1886 she ranked second to New York, the leading state. At present she holds the third place, North Carolina having surpassed her. The state has played a comparatively inconspicuous part in the cigar industry. In his Census Report of 1880, J. R. Dodge does not even reckon Virginia in his list of cigar states. The table below, prepared from the Census and Internal Revenue Reports, gives the comparative rank of the tobacco states for the years 1880 and 1890. The amount of raw material used and the tobacco consumed in the manufacture have been the criterion for determining relative superiority.

	In all products.		In plug and fine-cut, snuff and smoking.		In cigarettes.		In cigars.	
	1880.	1890.	1880.	1890.	1880.	1890.	1880.	1890.
1	Va.	Mo.	Va.	Mo.	....	N. Y.	N. Y.	Pa.
2	N. Y.	Va.	N. J.	Va.	....	N. C.	Pa.	N. Y.
3	N. J.	N. Y.	Mo.	N. J.	....	Va.	O.	O.
4	Mo.	N. J.	N. Y.	N. C.	....	La.	Ill.	Ill.
5	O.	N. C.	N. C.	Ky.	....	Md.	Cal.	Fla.
6	N. C.	O.	O.	O.	....	Cal.	Md.	Cal.
7	Pa.	Ky.	Ill.	N. Y.	....	O.	Mich.	Mich.
8	Ill.	Pa.	Ky.	Mich.	....	N. J.	Mass.	Mass.
9	Ky.	Md.	Md.	Md.	....	Pa.	Wis.	Md.
10	Mich.	Mich.	Mich.	Ill.	....	Fla.	Mo.	Wis.
11	Md.	Ill.	Wis.	Wis.	....	....	N. J.	Va.
12	Wis.	Wis.	Pa.	Pa.	....	Ill.	Ind.	N. J.
13	Cal.	La.	La.	W. Va.	....	Tex.	Fla.	Mont.
14	La.	Mass.	Del.	Tenn.	....	W. Va.	La.	Mo.
15	Del.	W. Va.	Mass.	La.	....	Mich.	Ky.	Ind.

CHAPTER VI.

THE HISTORY OF TOBACCO MANUFACTURE.

The periods of time taken for the study of Manufacture are identical with those for Production. The first period (1860-1871) was marked by a war and heavy taxation; the second (1871-1885) was marked by the monetary panic of 1873, the lowering of the tax, the influx of northern and foreign capital, and the rise of the cigarette and rehandling establishments; the third (1885-1894) was marked by reckless competition, the formation of the American Tobacco Company, and the panic of 1893.

SECTION I.—1860-1871.

Prior to the war the manufacture of tobacco was distributed throughout the whole tobacco-producing section of the state. Not only was a crude form of it found in the homes of the planters, but the tobacco factories were scattered throughout the country districts and were not confined alone to the cities and towns as at present. The towns were small, few railroads were built, the hands were hired for the year instead of by the day, the regular method for disposing of goods was through consignment to commission merchants, the general movement of the trade was slow, and under such conditions a country factory enjoyed almost the same advantages as a city factory, and its location would be determined as much by the nature of leaf grown in a particular section as by any other consideration. In 1860 there were 252 tobacco factories in Virginia. Of these, 109, as stated by the oldest manufacturers, were in Richmond, Petersburg, Lynchburg and Danville; the remaining 143 being distributed then throughout the country districts and among the small towns. Of the thirty generally recognized tobacco counties, there were nineteen which could claim manufactories.

But six or seven years after the war the country factories had all disappeared. In 1870 there were only 131 factories in the state, and 37 of these made "cigars and tobacco." Twelve counties which had, in 1860, 88 factories had only 17 in 1870, and seven counties which had 21 factories in the former year had none in the latter. Many city factories had also disappeared. Before the war Richmond had 50 factories, Lynchburg 35 and Danville 10; but after it Richmond had only 38, Lynchburg 16 and Danville 6.

There were two causes for the disappearance of the factories—the civil war and the heavy taxes. The oppressive effects of the latter were felt acutely because of the heavy losses sustained in the former. The war had left the manufacturers with their empty factories and rusted machinery, but with no labor, no money and with little credit. A few were fortunate enough to save during the war several hundred pounds of manufactured tobacco and were able to raise with this the necessary cash for paying taxes and continuing business, but the majority had only their knowledge and skill in the art of manufacture as capital to start with after the war, and had to depend entirely on the advances of their old commission merchants for taxes and running expenses. The tax originated in the act of July 1st, 1862, and went into effect the following September. At first it was deemed necessary for procuring revenue for carrying on the military operations of the government, and it was afterwards continued to provide for the payment of the debt and for pensions. The rate of taxation was not uniform. On different grades of manufactured tobacco it varied from 2 to 40 cts. per pound; on snuff from 20 to 40 cts. per pound; on cigars from $1.50 to $40.00 per thousand; on cigarettes from 40 cts. to $3.00 per thousand. Under some of the early laws the tax was made partly specific and partly *ad valorem*, with the view of bringing the quality and price of the goods in as elements determining the amount of the tax. This method was found to be impracticable, and later the stamp system was introduced, which was soon followed by the system of uniform taxation. The uniform tax has proved most satisfactory both to the manufacturer and to the internal revenue officers. It is easily complied with and easily collected. The uniform system was adopted on June 6th, 1872, and no other changes except those of repeated reductions have been made in the taxes since that time.

The effects of the different taxes have been numerous and interesting; they were not fully realized, however, for some years after they were first imposed, since it was as late as 1872 before they were thoroughly collected. Previous to this many factories had been evading the tax, and actually living on it as a profit, by imitating the inspector's stencil marks or by using repeatedly the same stamps on different packages. The country factories, and notably those in the mountain districts remote from the railroads, having a local trade supplied by wagons, paid little regard to the revenue laws, but like moonshiners making apple brandy, they believed that one stamp on a box or barrel could be made to answer all revenue requirements until it was completely worn out. Manufacturers in certain districts off the officer's beat were threatened with a raid if the proprietor did not at least make a show of buying stamps once a quarter to the extent of ten dollars' worth, to keep up an excuse for having internal revenue officers. The city manufacturers also found this blockading business a profitable one. All but four in Danville engaged in it, and one is reported as having sold tobacco in Baltimore at 40 cts. per pound when this figure barely covered the tax itself. This evasion of course seriously interfered with the business of honest manufacturers and its practice soon became very disreputable. By 1873 blockading had been practically abandoned altogether. But the form of the tax, being a graded one, furnished for some years another opportunity to cheat the Government, and manufacturers, as a class, availed themselves of it.

Before 1872 the tax on manufactured tobacco was uneven, there being two rates, 16 and 32 cts. per pound. It was the Government's intention that 32 cts. should be generally paid, the law stating that 16 cts. could only be paid on " smoking tobacco, made exclusively of stems, or of leaf with all the stems in it, and so sold; the leaf not having been previously stripped, butted, or rolled, and from which no part of the stems had been separated by sifting, stripping, or dressing, or in any other manner, either before, during, or after the process of manufacture." As this made the rate of the tax depend entirely on the process of manufacture it opened a wide door for fraud. The manufacturer would claim to cut his highest priced smoking tobacco, in the words of the law, " with all the stems in," and therefore refuse to pay more than 16 cts. to the pound. He also claimed to have the right to manufacture, cut or granulate his tobacco, the raw leaf even having been previously submitted to a process of sweetening, and, if the final product contained all or more than all of the stems natural to the leaf, to be entitled to sell it under the 16-cts. tax. Moreover, as the law required all chewing tobacco to pay 32 cts. per pound, the lowest grades of plug and twist were made to pay a tax double the amount of the one which the highest priced grades of smoking tobacco paid, notwithstanding the fact that the latter sold at double the price of the former; and as long cut smoking tobacco, especially when first sweetened, could be used instead of fine-cut for chewing purposes, some chewing tobacco was made to pay only 16 cts., while the cheapest grades of plug were always required to pay 32 cts. The difficulty of a fair collection of the tax lay in the fact that the manufacturer claimed that he had no possible way of telling whether his tobacco was to be used for chewing or smoking purposes. The introduction of the uniform system of taxation obviated this difficulty, and in the year following its adoption (1873) the unprecedented quantity of 114,789,208 pounds of tobacco in its various forms was returned for taxation, being a quantity in excess of the previous fiscal year of 19,579,889 pounds. The total revenue collections had decreased only $4\frac{1}{10}$ per cent., though there had been a reduction in the tax of $22\frac{1}{3}$ per cent.

Another unjust and discriminating effect of the tax was caused by the system of collection at the export warehouses. A law passed on July 20th, 1868, authorized the Commissioner of Internal Revenue to designate and establish at any port of entry in the United States warehouses for the storage of manufactured tobacco and snuff in bond, intended for exportation, while at the same time it authorized the collector in charge of exports to issue a permit for the withdrawal of such tobacco and snuff for consumption after the tax had been paid. There were established by this act 15 bonded warehouses: one in Boston, five in New York, four in Philadelphia, two in Baltimore, one in Richmond, one in New Orleans, and one in San Francisco. The provision in the law allowing the withdrawal of tobacco after the tax had been paid gave to the manufacturers selling in such cities the chance to use these export warehouses as storage rooms, and they began to place goods in bond which were in reality consigned to jobbers and were never intended for export. In 1871 less than half of the tobacco bonded was actually exported. From eight warehouses in Philadelphia, Baltimore, New Orleans, San Francisco and Portland (Oregon) only 437,495 pounds were exported, out of 9,437,257 pounds that were bonded. In 1870 only a little over two-fifths of that bonded was exported. The jobbers would wait until the market offered highest prices, pay the tax, withdraw the goods and sell them to their regular customers, receiving in this way about four or five months' credit and getting always the best prices that the market afforded. This advantage given by the Government to the jobbers in these seaport cities over those in other places caused much dissatisfaction. The demand was soon made by the merchants, as a class, that such warehouses should be established in all large cities or else they should be abolished altogether. The latter was done in 1872.

The many disturbances occasioned in the sensitive life of the industry by reason of the different agitations of the tax have been as numerous as the proposals and discussions of changes themselves, though the nature of these disturbances has always been the same. The regular effect on every occasion has been that the talk of lowering the tax has depressed manufacture for a time, and discussions as to raising it have always temporarily stimulated the industry.

But in addition to these general effects of the taxes felt by all manufacturers, certain effects were realized by those of Virginia as by those of no other state. The tax being very heavy and requiring a large bond, forced out of business men of limited means and concentrated manufacturing interests in the hands of the few who were able to raise from their commission merchants sufficient funds to meet the requirements. This favored the moneyed men and the moneyed states, and coming at a time when Virginia was financially depressed, resulted in effecting a virtual transfer from Virginia to other more wealthy states of a large part of her natural industry.

Section 2.—1871-1885.

By 1871 the manufacturers had recovered in a great measure from the losses sustained in the war. They had also become better used to the tax, had made some money, and had begun to enlarge their business and extend their trade. The next fourteen years were characterized by exceptional growth in all sorts of manufactures. There was only one factor in this period—the panic of 1873—which put any restraint upon the general development, and its evil effects were not sufficient to check for any considerable time the steady and rapid growth already begun.

The statistics of general manufactures for Virginia in the years 1870 and 1880 show well the remarkable growth in this whole period, and also the fact that there had been some little concentration in the business. There was a development of factory life along the new railways in the small towns but an abandonment of manufactures in the country districts, the country factory being unable to compete with the city factory having railroad facilities.

CENSUS STATISTICS OF MANUFACTURES FOR VIRGINIA, 1870–1880.

Years.	Capital Invested.	Hands Employed.	Wages.	Value of Material.	Value of Product.	Number of Establishments.
1870	$18,455,400	26,974	$5,343,099	$23,832,384	$38,364,322	5,933
1880	26,968,990	40,184	7,425,261	32,883,933	51,780,992	5,710

By the year 1880 the manufactures in Virginia were almost exactly 100 per cent. greater than they were in 1860; the capital invested had been doubled, the number of laborers employed had been more than doubled, and the gross amount of wages paid had increased about 80 per cent.[1] If the same ratio of increase had been maintained in the smaller towns as in the cities, it is probable that the manufactures throughout the state in 1885 would have been little, if at all, short of 200 per cent. greater than they were in 1870. In certain leading branches of manufacture, and in particular in tobacco in all its forms of manipulation, the increase was enormous. In the year 1884 the following enterprises were undertaken: in Richmond a $75,000 cigarette factory; in Roanoke, a $15,000 tobacco factory, and in Danville, two aggregating $35,000. Since 1875 several tobacco establishments had grown up in Goodson, Abingdon, South Boston, Martinsville, Bedford City, Chatham, Chase City and like towns. Virginia had in 1870 131 factories, of which 94 were for " manufactured tobacco " and 37 made " tobacco and cigars "; in 1880 it had 199 factories, of

[1] " Virginia: Geographical and Political Summary." Maj. Jed. Hotchkiss.

which 143 were for "manufactured tobacco" and 56 for "tobacco, cigars and cigarettes." The statistics for several counties show the same development.[1]

With this general growth, we note also the rise of two new and distinct branches of the industry, viz., the reprizing business and cigarette manufacture. The first represented only a further division of labor, the second was an entirely new industry. The object of rehandling establishments was to prepare leaf tobacco for manufacturers and shippers by stemming it, sorting it into different classes and putting it in fine keeping order. The process of stemming, prizing and ordering did not change the quality of the leaf, although it could be made to give desirable color to certain grades, especially suited to foreign trade and sometimes demanded by the home factories for special brands. No account was taken of these establishments in the census of 1870, but, in 1880, 27 were given to the state, and in 1890 the number had increased to 101. The development of cigarette manufacture was discussed in the chapter on Production, as well as the causes of the extraordinary growth of manufactures in this period.

Section 3.—1885-1894.

The first half of this period is marked by the disappearance of many of the factories which had been built during the preceding one. The factories in the small towns could not compete with those in the cities; Virginia had only 93 factories for "manufactured tobacco" in 1890, whereas

---

[1] Table, from census reports of 1870-1880, giving number of factories for "manufactured tobacco" with annual product valued at over $500.00.

COUNTIES.	1870.	1880.
Bedford	5	7
Halifax	0	3
Henry	4	14
Roanoke	0	6
Pittsylvania	8	29

she had 143 in 1880. All the small factories having been forced out of business by 1890, the latter half of this period is called the period of large factories, and it is characterized by "cut-throat" competition in the marketing of goods.

The competition has taken the form of special bribes, gifts and inducements from the manufacturers to the trade, which have burdened them with so much expense that their business hardly returns any margin of profit. In establishing a new brand, the manufacturer must first offer special inducements to the jobber to take hold of the goods, the freight must be paid and a certain amount of tobacco given him; then he must offer the retailer a step-ladder or a clock for every five caddies sold, and the consumer a pocket-knife or dinner-pail on presentation of a specified number of plug tags. More than this, he must employ the mail and distribute free samples of his goods all over the country and must send his agents to the foundries, mines and factories with valises full of tobacco to give to the laborers in order to create a demand for his new brands. The gifts and advertising require as much skill as the manufacturing business itself and more worry, and to conduct these departments successfully the proprietor would do well to ally himself with a furniture factory or chromo establishment. Indeed manufacturers have gone further. After offering numerous schemes with costly prizes to the jobbers and retailers, they have begun to bribe the salesmen of these parties, and to give the jobber's travelling agent, as well as the retailer's clerk, a special pro rata bonus on the goods sold, and thus have cheated these employers out of a part of their salesmen's time. The jobbers have seen the wrong done them by such action on the part of the manufacturers and have done their best to stop such unprincipled conduct. The papers make mention of Merchants' Associations all over the country framing resolutions denouncing this nefarious business.

But more than this, sharp competition has occasioned a

system of cutting prices among plug manufacturers which has resulted in almost ruining their business. The price of good plug tobacco averages from 30 to 75 cents per pound, but in the summer of 1893 it was being offered by a few leading factories at 13 cents and less. The tax was 6 cents, which left only 7 cents to pay for the leaf, manufacture, freight charges, etc.; the cost of raising a pound of leaf is 6 cents. If there was any profit to the manufacturer in this there could certainly be none to the planter. In the spring of 1894, 17-cent plug and less ruled the market, with gifts thrown in. And not only were prices cut to consumers, but the price for the jobbers was "jockeyed" with. The manufacturer published from time to time his card list prices and he was under contract to sell his brands at these prices to every merchant doing business for him, but by giving certain amounts of tobacco to some and not to others, by prepayment of freight or by extending credit, he discriminated among them. The jobbers have opposed these methods as unnecessary and unfair "tricks of trade."

The results of free competition here do not seem altogether satisfactory. The jobber and the retailer are dissatisfied, the consumer is cheated, the price of leaf is depressed, and the manufacturer is forced to use unjust and unbusiness-like methods to make a bare living. There seems to be an absolute necessity for having some organization or understanding to prevent ruinous competition and unfair methods. The question resolves itself into this: must there be a trust at fixed prices, or free competition and irregular prices? No matter what prices one manufacturer may establish at the factory, unrestricted competition will soon demoralize them, for when he would compel a profit others will insist on selling their goods below cost. Without some restriction or agreement it is impossible to establish and maintain prices, and when such an agreement is had it virtually constitutes a monopoly. The history of the American Tobacco Company will be of interest at this point.

This company was formed in 1890[1]; it was first the union of Allen & Ginter in Richmond, the Kinney Tobacco Company of New York, W. Duke Sons & Co. of Durham, N. C. and of New York City, Wm. S. Kimball & Co., Rochester, N. Y., Goodwin & Co. of N. Y., and soon embraced also Marburg Bros. and Gail & Ax of Baltimore. Some idea of its size, growth and power can be gained from one of its annual reports.[2] The enormous profits and the large advertising fund indicate that the purpose of the combination has not been simply to save costs in marketing goods but also to get full control of the entire cigarette industry. The organization has succeeded in accomplishing this, for it is said to control about 90 per cent. of all the cutters marketed and 95 per cent. of all the cigarettes sold. The company controls the cigarette trade by offering extraordinary inducements to the jobbers and retailers who promise to handle its own goods exclusively; it has controlled cigarette manufacture in a large measure by

[1] The American Tobacco Company cannot legitimately be called a trust, though it passes for one in the tobacco terminology of all newspapers, for it owns outright the brands, trade-marks, goodwill, property, etc., consisting of tobacco and manufacturing supplies, and its existence can only be terminated by such liquidations as would be necessary to the discontinuance of the business of any banking, insurance, or other corporation. Its charter was obtained from the New Jersey legislature, after it had been applied for in the Virginia legislature, given, and then repealed.

[2] The net earnings for the year 1893, after deducting all charges and expenses for management, etc., were $4,334,467.34, out of which the Company had declared four quarterly dividends of 2 per cent. each on the preferred stock, amounting to $956,800, leaving $3,377,667.34 to be applied to its surplus account and the payment of dividends on its common stock. The surplus account, as shown December 31, 1892, was $4,107,895.31, which with this year's $3,377,667.34, makes a total of $7,485,562.65, out of which there has been declared a 12 per cent. dividend on its common stock, amounting to $2,152,500, leaving a net surplus, December 31, 1893, of $5,333,062.65, being a net increase over that of December 31, 1892, of $1,225,167.34. The total assets of the Company were $37,168,253.13, the total liabilities $29,835,000.00, and the advertising fund was $477,969.44.

leases, for this country alone, of the most important and practical cigarette machines, among which are the Allison, the Bohl, the Bonsack and the Luddington.

The liveliest opposition in a competitive way that the company has ever encountered came from the National Cigarette and Tobacco Company of New York, incorporated in June of 1892 with a capital of $2,500,000. This company had much success with the Elliott machine, which proved the equal, if not the superior, of the Bonsack, the leading machine of the American Tobacco Company. The National Company soon cost the American Tobacco Company about $300,000 in advertising, and the competition was so sharp that the Bonsack Machine Company found it necessary to stop the Elliott machine or else consider its contract with the American Tobacco Company null and void.[1] The Bonsack Company at once sued the Elliott Machine Company for infringement of patent, and it gained in June 12, 1894, from Judge Lacombe of the United States Circuit Court for the Southern District of New York, the order that the National Company should suspend operations until the next court. The National gave bond, however, and continued to manufacture until another court was held, at which time the decision was reversed and the Elliott machine was set free. A popular belief exists that an open market for cigarette machines would be the solution of a successful competition with the American Tobacco Company.[2]

In addition to its enormous cigarette industry, the American Tobacco Company owns also a considerable share in

---

[1] It is said that the Bonsack Machine Company receives something like $250,000 a year from the American Tobacco Company for furnishing protection from new machines.—" Southern Tobacconist and Manufacturer's Record."

[2] Since 1894 the Company has allowed its leases on all machines to expire, and at this time (1896) the Bonsack and other machines are in use in competitive factories, yet the Company still holds its own.

the plug manufacture[1] of the country, and in this branch of the trade it is claimed that much damage has been done to tobacco manufacturers by sacrificing tobacco in order to get a wider sale for its cigarettes. Many jobbers who once sold tobacco for several different factories handle now the American Tobacco Company's, because the company gives them particularly low prices and large inducements for handling its goods exclusively. The tobacco manufacturers have complained a great deal of this and they talk at present of forming a great combination, composed of the largest plug factories in the country, viz., the Brown Company, Liggett & Myers, the Drummond Company, and the Catlin Tobacco Company; the purpose of which shall be to fight the American Tobacco Company by manufacturing cigarettes and sacrificing these in order to sell plug tobacco. If this " Anti-trust Cigarette Factory," as it is termed, is organized, this with the National Tobacco and Cigarette Company should create for the American Tobacco Company a lively competition.[2]

The American Tobacco Company employs very exacting contracts with its agents and consignees in regard to the methods to be used in the conduct of its business.. Its numerous and explicit rules have proven annoying to some jobbers, and have subjected the company to the criticism of being unnecessarily dictatorial; to others, however, the plan has been very acceptable and has met with entire approval. Southern jobbers, in whose business the sale of cigarettes forms only a small and unimportant part, dislike the method, while those in the large, prosperous cities, north, east, and west, who handle cigarettes in large quantities, favor it. The company claims that the plan is em-

---

[1] Since the company's organization it has purchased the National Tobacco Works of Louisville, Ky., and the J. G. Butler Co. of St. Louis.

[2] Already cigarettes are being manufactured and aggressively pushed by Liggett & Myers, and the Drummond Tobacco Co. of St. Louis.

ployed to protect the jobber against reckless cutting of prices, rather than to gain any special benefit for itself. Prices, penalties, commissions, etc., are all fixed by the company, in its agencies, or consignments, and few jobbers prosper in the cigarette business who do not accept the agency plan as the company gives it. If the company finds one of its agents selling under contract prices, it has the right reserved to call without notice for the balance of goods on hand and this agency is then closed, the agent receiving a check for the company's stock. The company minimizes its loss in case of an agent's failure by the consignment clause in its contract which allows the company to take all goods unsold and unsettled for.

The third and last subject for consideration within this period is the long and severe panic of 1893. For at least nine months of this year there was entire stagnation in every branch of the tobacco industry, and for at least eighteen months the output of all the factories was restricted. As late as June, 1894, the manufacturers were doing only a " hand to mouth " business, aiming to have just enough stock on hand to supply temporary demand and to keep their brands before the public. However, they pulled through the panic with as little loss probably as any other class of business men; a few enjoyed the fostering care of the banks, and all could save themselves in part by turning off hands and cutting down expenses. It was to the interest of the banks to be very careful with their customer's credit. Having received tobacco notes and securities during the summer of 1893, which they saw were not marketable for anything like their par value when priced at auction, they realized that they had actual property possessions and held them for better times, when a revival of trade would redeem them at something like their full value. In this way the tobacco markets and manufacturers tided over the summer, and were not thrown into chaos by failures due to the strained finances of the period. Indeed a few large plug factories worked the full time, through the panic, by virtue of their large capital and cash selling. In the latter part of 1894 and the beginning of 1895 the revival of trade set in, but with this revival came also the necessity of final settlements, and as this demand proved too hard for some factories a few failures occurred. The sale of old stocks which had depreciated in value by reason of age, in a market where stocks had been accumulating for almost three years, did not return sufficient money for meeting old debts and current expenses, and the consequence was that several manufacturers went to the wall. The low price of cotton and the American Tobacco Company probably had as much to do with their failure as the contracted money market. Nine or ten manufacturers were bankrupt in the state during the whole period, and in the leaf trade, which had been drifting more and more into the hands of a few agents for large corporations, about one-third of the middlemen were driven out. The wages for factory hands remained the same throughout the panic and no strikes occurred.

CHAPTER VII.

The Manufacturer.

Section 1.—What has he to say about the taxes, the American Tobacco Company, and unrestricted competition?

As the taxes had been imposed to pay the expenses of a war in which Virginia had lost all her wealth and so large a proportion of her population, they would hardly be welcomed by Virginia manufacturers. All Virginians hated the tax, and many of the old manufacturers even now manifest intense indignation when discussing it. They feel that the tax was imposed on tobacco by the Union because the South and Virginia, which produced most of it, were largely responsible through the war for its necessity. They have steadily fought to lower it, and have succeeded in reducing it from 40 to 6 cts. As this is not burdensome, some willingly bear it, and a few manufacturers who have large capital would even prefer that the tax were higher still, since it would shut out some competitors. However, as a class, manufacturers would remove it entirely and would vote for a full divorcement of the government from the industry, since the agitation of the tax has invariably done such serious injury to the business.

To the plug manufacturer, the American Tobacco Company is a sure evil. There may be redeeming features about it for the consumer, retailer, jobber and planter, but there are none for him. The more of his business it destroys by its liberal gifts to the trade the better it is liked by the public; the people are gratified, but the manufacturer suffers.

To rid themselves of the evils of unscrupulous competition, the manufacturers have repeatedly agreed among themselves to maintain regular prices which would insure to all a reasonable profit, but as the fulfillment of such contracts was left entirely to the honor and pleasure of each individual, and since no penalty was incurred by a breach of promise, these contracts were broken as often as made. The heavy costs and small profits resulting from unrestricted competition is forcing them to consider more and more the advantages of combination and co-operation; the tendency to consolidate is growing stronger every day.

Section 2.—To what extent has the manufacturer organized, and what has he accomplished by it?

As soon as the tobacco interests of a place develop, a local trade association is formed. This comprises on its roll all the leading leaf dealers, brokers and manufacturers. The purpose of the association is to advance the tobacco interests of the place by having joint counsel among its members in regulating the sale of loose tobacco at the warehouses, in securing equitable rates of freight, and in exercising such supervisory authority over all transactions as shall secure perfectly fair play between buyer and seller.

Under the Tobacco Association are different boards, as the " Manufacturers Board " and the " Tobacco Warehouse Board." The first is composed exclusively of manufacturers, and its purpose and province are limited to what may be called domestic or interior interests, such as fixing the scale of wages to be paid to the factory operatives. The object of the " Warehouse Board " is to agree upon an uniform system for conducting their general affairs and to protect the warehouseman's interests from outside adverse influences.

With such organizations it is very easy for tobacconists to bring their united influence and power to bear at once for the accomplishment of any end. By this union of effort they have directed law-making both in state legislature and in Congress; in the latter they have repeatedly lowered the tax; in the former they have changed the warehouse system and the inspection laws.

Before the year 1872 the fact of having an uneven and graded tax gave the manufacturers much annoyance, and to gain the adoption of a uniform tax they endeavored to influence Congress through the General Assembly, which body they could reach through their associations. On February 20, 1872, the following resolutions were forwarded to Congress urging this reform:

"Whereas the unsettled state of the question of the tax upon tobacco has caused an almost total suspension of the tobacco manufacturing interests; and whereas, in consequence thereof a very large and indigent class of laborers, embracing at least 30,000 operatives, and those dependent on them, have been deprived of employment and the means of subsistence, thereby causing great distress and suffering among them, they being for the most part unsuited for any other employment; and whereas other branches of industry which are dependent upon the business of tobacco manufacture are like it, stagnated and paralyzed; and whereas, in the opinion of the General Assembly of this State, a uniform instead of graded tax upon tobacco would be highly beneficial to the trade in preventing fraud, and in doing justice to the plug tobacco manufacturers of the entire country, they being the largest class of manufacturers in said business of tobacco manufacture; therefore, first,

"Resolved, That the General Assembly of Virginia do most earnestly request the Congress of the United States to take up and at once act upon the question of the tax upon tobacco by enacting a uniform rate of tax upon all grades and descriptions of manufactured tobacco and snuff at the lowest possible rate consistent with the interests of the general government.

"Second, that the Senators from this state be instructed, and Representatives requested, to use their influence and vote for in the Congress of the United States the passage of such a law at the earliest possible moment."

We find that in the following June, Congress passed a law which changed the tax to a uniform one of 20 cts. The numerous reductions effected in the tax, which have occurred in as many as 12 or 15 different years, have all been preceded by like resolutions from the tobacconists and the General Assembly.

The change from the system of state warehouses to that of private warehouses and of inspectors appointed by the Government to those appointed by the trade was also brought about through the manufacturers' associations. In the legislature of 1874-1875 the manufacturers and warehousemen of Richmond had made their first earnest effort to get this important change, but they had failed because of the strong opposition offered at the time by the planters, who believed that the trade was trying to divorce the business from the state in order to manipulate charges to its own interest and to the injury of the tobacco-growers. But though the Richmond men were defeated at this time, they were not the less determined to gain their point; so that they renewed the contest in the session of 1877-78, and finally succeeded in making the desired changes.

Such have been some of the results accomplished by organization among the manufacturers. They have succeeded in this way in advancing their interests not only by joint counsel, but also by much favorable legislation and some concessions in railroad rates.

Section 3.—Relation of the manufacturer to his market.

The general relation of the manufacturer to his market is that of subordination; his time and money are spent in finding the wants of his buyers, and if once he learns their wishes he will surely cater to them. He is bound by no iron-clad custom. He is glad to answer any call of the trade, whether it be for cheap or high-priced tobacco, mild or strong, bright or black. In many instances he has acted as the employee of the jobber, who has hired him to supply special brands, particularly well suited to the jobber's own trade, over whose prices the jobber is to have full control.

But the manufacturer is in some measure master of his market too; by creating new wants he can give direction to the demand. When the trade seems to have no special preferences he may get out a brand that pleases every one, that becomes fashionable and popular, and in this way by creating a new demand may give direction and character

to consumption. Since he knows that tastes can be cultivated, he takes as much care in the concoction of his
flavorings as the confectioner does in mixing his candies,
and in so far as he is able to create a decided preference for
his own special flavorings, just so far is he liable to get wide
sales and to make extraordinary profits. He recognizes
also that the appearance and name of a thing, as well as
its quality, has much to do with its sale, so he appeals to
both the eye and ear in placing his goods before the public.
A cigarette drummer affirms that one-half the battle in
establishing a new brand is the selection of a euphonious
name, and the pleasing names given to all classes of tobacco
would certainly argue that there was some truth in the
statement.[1]

But not only is the manufacturer master of his market in
the sense that he can make decided changes in demand and
can give special directions to consumption, but also in the
sense that he largely creates and supports the entire general
demand that exists at any one time. He starts with the
consumer and makes the trade for all the intermediate agents
which comprise his selling market, and he has the power, on
well established brands, to contract or enlarge his trade in
a degree at will through the manipulation of prices and the
offering of special inducements. His largest chance for
profit lies in this control of selling prices, by which he can
extend his market and force out small competitors, and not,
as many planters believe, in the continued reduction of
prices on leaf.

Section 4.—What has been the manufacturer's explanation
of the low prices for leaf tobacco?

---

[1] Note a few of them: for cigarettes, " Pearl's Pet," " Trio's Delight," " Old Soldier," " City Talk "; for cigars and cheroots,
" Cuban Dainties," " Centennial Pets," " Little Darlings "; for
plug, " Dwarf Roses," " Peach and Honey," " Pioneer's Delight,"
" Sweet Reverie," " Just the Thing," " Take-a-Chew "; for smoking tobacco, " Farmer's Choice," " Old Rip," " Fruits and Flow-
ers," " Virginia Creeper," " Planter's Pride," etc.

He has given eight reasons, more or less distinct:

1. Over-production of inferior grades.

2. The planter's ignorance of the demands of the market; no aim to make special grades; too much nondescript.

3. Excessive use of commercial fertilizers, which have stimulated too rapidly the growth of tobacco and have injured it by not giving the plant time to mature.

4. The soil not suited to the variety grown.

5. Poor culture and rough handling, due to leaving the care of the crop to negro tenants.

6. Impoverished soil employed without the assistance of good manures or fertilizers.

7. New and inexperienced farmers trying the crop in other states.

8. An increased production of tobacco in foreign countries.

CHAPTER VIII.

CONCLUSIONS.

From the foregoing discussion of the entire subject we think we may safely draw the following conclusions:

1. General prices of tobacco have materially declined in recent years; the decline is due in part to the farmer's poor methods of culture and curing, but in the main to causes beyond his control—general over-production in all the states and in foreign countries, this being considered a cause beyond the control of the farmers of a single state, such as Virginia.

2. Low prices have caused some restriction of tobacco acreage and some diversification of crops.

3. It will no longer pay to raise tobacco to the exclusion of other crops; fine tobacco still returns a handsome profit to the planter, but as only fine tobacco which meets special demand pays, there exists imperative necessity for further specialization in production.

4. Farmers' organizations have proved successful; they have been much more helpful to their members as business organizations than as political ones. There exists, however, in an alliance of farmers the possibility of exercising great political power.

5. Many successful farmers have been materially aided by patronizing the Farmers Institutes and by reading agricultural papers.

6. The manufacturer studies his market closely.

7. The general policy of manufacturers is to organize; their associations have been highly beneficial.

8. Unequal and unjust tax laws have encouraged dishonest practices.

9. The evils of unrestricted competition seem quite as pernicious as those of trusts.

10. Against the American Tobacco Company it may be said:

(*a*) It has lowered the price of leaf tobacco.

(*b*) It has injured the manufacturer's leaf market by monopolizing certain classes and leaving less variety to select from.

(*c*) It has injured his selling market by sacrificing tobacco to sell cigarettes.

(*d*) It has checked the natural development of competitive cigarette factories by acquiring control of the most important cigarette machines.

(*e*) Having almost entire control of the trade, it has been able to determine prices arbitrarily on many popular brands.

For the company it may be said:

(*a*) By its large advertisement both in the United States and foreign countries it has built up an immense market for cigarettes, and this has well sustained the price on cutters.

(*b*) The jobber and retailer have received a fair commission when consenting to do business in the company's own way.

(*c*) The consumer has been given a very acceptable grade of cigarette at a reasonably low price.

(*d*) As an advantage to the citizens of Richmond, it may be added that its immense business builds up the place where its factories are located in a way commensurate with its great enterprise, furnishing employment to hundreds of operatives and making very considerable contribution to the city's taxes.

Year.	Per ct. U. S. Inter. Revenue paid by Virginia.	Per ct. total Rev. from Tobacco paid by Virginia.	Amount Revenue from Virginia Tobacco.	Amount Internal Revenue paid by Virginia.
1864	.126	.073	$	$ 137,513.72
1865	.112	.110	12,517.34	221,273.39
1866	.405	1.451	238,873.28	1,175,447.50
1867	.793	1.510	283,437.32	1,966,722.02
1868	1.018	2.269	423,521.31	1,783,319.60
1869	1.919	6.512	1,525,912.45	2,744,144.45
1870	3.280	12.977	4,068,220.78	5,496,351.39
1871	4.160	12.996	4,363,911.17	5,319,272.69
1872	4.284	11.797	3,980,005.03	4,939,027.93
1873	6.912	19.098	6,567,039.68	7,343,799.29
1874	6.547	17.157	5,703,425.66	6,308,664.96
1875	7.383	18.871	7,039,615.15	7,660,921.20
1876	6.606	17.467	6,951,119.77	7,314,393.64
1877	7.048	18.163	7,465,982.94	7,932,220.78
1878	6.209	15.328	6,145,442.85	6,501,730.29
1879	6.015	15.228	6,111,908.26	6,448,546.88
1880	4.948	13.806	5,366,272.82	5,781,409.58
1881	4.742	13.220	5,665,369.58	6,063,105.75
1882	4.480	12.237	5,799,346.76	6,226,308.30
1883	3.693	11.259	4,740,352 52	5,078,146.35
1884	2.664	11.048	2,879,374.21	3,232,726.10
1885	2.715	10.266	2,710,814.20	3,052,639.72
1886	2.551	9.434	2,632,896.59	2,982,727.70
1887	2.460	8.633	2,599,136.12	2,923,394.64
1888	2.617	9.616	2,948,620.12	3,253,165.72
1889	2.524	9.435	3,006,520.83	3,303,626.48
1890	2.466	9.410	3,195,382.22	3,516,195.49
1891	2.197	8.763	2,873,914.60	3,208,066.34
1892	1.895	8.132	2,520,940.99	2,915,412.52
1893	1.809	8.080	2,576,934.65	2,912,548.28
1894	1.731	7.559	2,163,146.99	2,548,051.75

TOBACCO MANUFACTURED—TOTALS FOR VIRGINIA.

	Plug, Pounds.	Fine Cut.	Smoking.	Snuff.	TOTAL.	On Hand.	Total to be Accounted For.	On Hand, Unsold.	Exported in Bond.	Sold.	Stamps required for Sales.
1880	39,393,994	2,211	1,275,569	6,133		924,157	42,602,066				
1881	43,925,784		1,405,479	6,609		751,014	46,088,886				
1882	36,500,299		1,158,951	11,979		748,616	38,419,846		9,989,335		
1883	45,129,962		1,164,156	23,262	46,317,380	9,074,507	55,239,837	9,707,026	7,915,774	37,952,034	$3,521,989.80
1884	35,630,657		783,283	73,028	36,486,968	9,420,897	45,907,865	8,209,177	7,604,637	30,094,051	2,409,243.32
1885	44,086,437		1,222,923	17,050	45,226,410	8,978,626	54,205,036	11,545,173	10,019,765	32,640,098	2,611,207.81
1886	38,238,063		903,353	112,019	39,253,435	11,637,496	50,890,931	12,965,608	9,121,774	28,803,549	2,304,283.92
1887	35,670,004		1,386,825	168,473	37,225,302	12,184,378	49,409,680	9,130,032	8,715,855	31,563,793	2,525,103.44
1888	37,011,355		1,339,792	337,725	38,688,872	9,019,428	47,708,300	7,705,370	10,038,192	29,964,738	2,397,179.04
1889	42,899,807	9,575	1,385,196	759,450	45,054,028	8,167,719	53,221,747	9,938,584	10,168,487	33,114,676	2,649,174.08
1890	34,624,504	72,783	1,932,890	729,768	37,359,945	9,641,777	47,001,722	7,915,392	8,907,572	30,178,758	2,414,300.64
1891	38,729,912		2,910,019	776,397	42,416,328	8,630,869	50,947,197	8,778,578	9,480,263	32,688,356	1,961,301.36
1892	34,089,859		3,538,559	776,517	38,404,935	8,246,394	46,651,329	8,170,199	8,550,583	29,930,547	1,795,832.82
1893	30,316,865		3,667,991	583,200	34,568,056	8,330,182	42,898,238	7,850,575	8,645,975	26,401,688	1,584,101.28

VIRGINIA—CIGARS AND CIGARETTES.

	No. of Factories having one account.	Pounds of Tobacco used.	Pounds used in Cigars.	Pounds used in Cigarettes.	No. Cigars Manufactured.	No. Cigarettes Manufactured.
1877	148	236,467			9,851,107	
1878						
1879						
1880	141	613,994			19,378,344	52,259,440
1881	132	754,107			22,669,345	69,498,590
1882	160		788,888 (Both Cigars and Cigarettes.)		24,276,884	88,722,350
1883	153	922,332			29,331,753	116,846,245
1884	186	998,675			57,595,761 } (Both Cigars and Cigarettes.)	
1885	172	1,123,742			40,330,464	
1886	168	1,264,520			24,778,395	273,344,710
1887	181	1,885,180			35,524,498	384,704,210
1888	199		2,484,022 (Both Cigars and Cigarettes.)		44,966,938	530,842,000
1889	216	2,808,738			65,679,118	566,130,000
1890	204	3,049,356			85,370,577	591,795,880
1891	227		1,516,000	1,655,646	104,771,522	647,073,560
1892	217		2,309,459	1,974,275	130,836,613	750,314,753
1893	265		1,527,589	3,019,931	103,482,527	802,929,195

REVENUE OF THE UNITED STATES FROM TOBACCO.

	Manufactured.	Snuff.	Cigars and Cheroots.	Cigarettes.	Total for Tobacco.	Per ct. of tot'l rec'pts com'g from Tobacco.	Average rate tax per lb.
1863	$2,578,972.43		$ 476,589.29		$3,097,620.47		.10 8/100
1864	7,086,684.74		1,255,424.74		8,592,098.98	7.33	.11 1/100
1865	8,017,020.63		3,072,476.56		11,401,373.10	5.40	.22 18/100
1866	12,339,921.93		3,474,438.94		16,531,007.83	5.32	.34 77/100
1867	15,245,477.81		3,661,984.39		19,765,148.41	7.43	.33 10/100
1868	14,947,107.53		2,951,675.26		18,730,095.32	9.80	.33 86/100
1869					23,430,707.57	14.64	.33 10/100
1870	24,300,483.42		5,718,780.04		31,350,707.88	16.92	.27 10/100
1871	25,560,539.61		6,598,173.24		33,578,907.18	23.31	.26 10/100
1872	18,674,569.26	$5,896,206.33	7,566,156.86		33,736,170.52	25.60	.26 8/100
1873	22,311,398.15	1,086,460.07	8,940,391.48		34,386,303.09	30.14	.25 8/100
1874	20,900,509.67	1,038,445.92	9,333,592.24		33,242,875.62	32.39	.20 10/100
1875	24,133,726.48	1,067,033.03	10,205,827.53		37,303,461.88	33.75	.20 8/100
1876	25,694,312.56	1,061,467.64	10,969,787.28	$135,485.17	39,795,339.91	33.94	.21 10/100
1877	27,053,072.38	1,095,695.52	11,061,278.15	289,081.79	41,106,546.92	34.54	.24 24/100
1878	25,320,158.08	1,063,714.22	11,430,144.60	416,984.43	40,091,754.67	36.09	.24 24/100
1879	24,703,874.90	902,135.35	12,115,468.39	715,269.39	40,135,002.65	35.23	.24 10/100
1880	21,170,154.40	634,609.34	14,206,819.49	992,981.22	38,870,140.08	31.22	.21 27/100
1881	22,833,287.60	689,183.03	16,095,724.78	992,981.22	42,854,991.31	31.56	.16
1882	25,033,741.97	778,650.78	18,245,852.37	972,570.10	47,391,988.91	32.22	.16
1883	22,136,402.53	736,022.82	16,895,215.15	929,974.73	42,104,249.79	29.00	.13 42/100
1884	13,488,047.41	448,211.58	10,368,805.27	454,409.01	26,062,399.98	21.43	.08
1885	13,953,400.31	508,943.52	10,077,287.50	529,535.88	26,407,088.48	23.49	.08
1886	14,834,095.42	493,283.80	10,532,804.05	655,569.55	27,907,362.53	23.87	.08
1887	15,995,019.46	524,942.26	11,364,916.33	792,279.60	30,108,067.13	25.34	.08
1888	16,154,049.05	594,950.13	11,534,179.95	931,363.05	30,662,431.52	24.66	.08
1889					31,886,860.42	24.35	.08
1890	18,325,481.36	737,731.27	12,263,669.95	1,116,627.34	33,958,991.06	23.82	.08
1891	17,080,632.67	726,155.39	13,424,678.30	1,342,269.38	32,796,270.97	22.46	.07 10/100
1892	15,237,742.32	669,861.08	13,646,398.25	1,446,491.42	31,000,493.07	20.15	.06
1893	15,143,981.91	714,773.63	14,442,591.35	1,588,361.85	31,889,711.74	19.80	.06
1894	14,127,108.31	697,625.52	12,200,752.30	1,592,412.49	28,617,898.62	19.45	.06
							13.53

BIBLIOGRAPHY.

1. "Internal Commerce of United States—Report on Virginia." By J. D. Imboden.

2. "Virginia: Geographical and Political Summary." By Major Jed Hotchkiss.

3. "Hand-books of Virginia" for years 1879, 1881. By Thos. Pollard.

4. "Virginia: A Hand-book," 1893. By Thos. Whitehead.

5. "Tobacco in Tennessee." By J. B. Killebrew.

6. Reports of Agricultural Department of Virginia from 1888 to '93.

7. Reports of U. S. Commissioner of Agriculture from 1867 to '93.

8. Reports of Chamber of Commerce in Richmond, Va., for years 1889, 1891 and 1893.

9. Internal Revenue Reports from 1861 to 1894.

10. Census reports for 1860, 1870, 1880, 1890, with Special Reports on Tobacco in the Census of 1880. By J. R. Dodge and J. B. Killebrew.

11. "Sketch Book of Danville: Its Manufacture and Commerce." By Edward Pollock. 1885.

12. "The City on the James, Richmond, Va." By Andrew Morrison. 1891.

13. "The position tobacco has ever held to the state of Virginia as her chief source of wealth." A circular published in 1876 by Southern Fertilizer Company of Richmond, Va., and written by John Ott, its Secretary.

14. "Centennial Souvenir of Lynchburg, Va." By Hinton A. Helper. 1886.

15. "Southern Tobacconist and Manufacturer's Record." Edited in Richmond, Va., by Wm. E. Dibrell. 1890-1894.

16. "The Southern Planter." Edited in Richmond, Va., by J. T. Jackson. 1867-1894.

17. "The Tobacco Journal" of Danville, Va. Edited by D. E. Graham.

www.ingramcontent.com/pod-product-compliance
Lightning Source LLC
Chambersburg PA
CBHW021426090426
42742CB00009B/1283

*9 7 8 3 3 3 7 3 3 8 8 9 3 *